THEMES
for early years

AUTUMN

JANICE FILER

THEMES
for early years

Author Janice Filer
Editors Jane Bishop and Susan Howard
Assistant editor Lesley Sudlow
Series designer Lynne Joesbury
Designer Mark Udall
Illustrations Kim Woolley
Cover Lynne Joesbury
Action Rhymes, Poems and Stories compiled by Jackie Andrews
Songs compiled by Peter Morrell
Assemblies chapter by Lesley Prior

Designed using Adobe Pagemaker
Processed by Scholastic Ltd, Leamington Spa

Published by Scholastic Ltd, Villiers House, Clarendon Avenue, Leamington Spa, Warwickshire CV32 5PR

The publishers gratefully acknowledge permission to reproduce the following copyright material:

Jackie Andrews for 'Mrs Rabbit's Autumn Pie' © 1999, Jackie Andrews, previously unpublished; Clive Barnwell for 'Mister Autumn' and 'Colour me Autumn' © 1999, Clive Barnwell, previously unpublished; Kirsty Bilton for 'When does Autumn Begin?' © 1999, Kirsty Bilton, previously unpublished; Ann Bryant for 'Time to say Goodbye' © 1999, Ann Bryant, previously unpublished; Sue Cowling for 'I'm a Little Conker!' and 'New Taste Festival' © 1999, Sue Cowling, previously unpublished; Susan Eames for 'One little acorn' and 'Flying away' © 1999, Susan Eames, previously unpublished; Jean Gilbert for 'Signs of Autumn' © 1999, Jean Gilbert, previously unpublished; Jillian Harker for 'Jake's Tree' © 1999, Jillian Harker, previously unpublished; Trevor Harvey for 'Autumn Carpet' © 1999, Trevor Harvey, previously unpublished; Carole Henderson-Begg for 'Harvest' © 1999, Carole Henderson-Begg, previously unpublished; Penny Kent for 'Autumn Bonfire' © 1999, Penny Kent, previously unpublished; Jean Kenward for 'Lanterns' © 1999, Jean Kenward, previously unpublished; Karen King for 'Falling Leaves' © 1999, Karen King, previously unpublished; Tony Mitton for 'Squirrel Store' (A Counting Rhyme), 'Here are the Trees', 'The Fruit Rhyme' © 1999, Tony Mitton, previously unpublished; Belinda Morley for 'Pick! Pluck! Pull!' © 1999, Belinda Morley, previously unpublished; Peter Morrell for 'God's Wonderful World' © 1999, Peter Morrell, previously unpublished; Judith Nicholls for 'Sycamore Seed' from *Higgledy Humbug* by Judith Nicholls © 1990, Judith Nicholls (1990, Mary Glasgow Publications); Coral Rumble for 'One Little Hedgehog' and 'Dandelion Whispers' © 1999, Coral Rumble, previously unpublished; Celia Warren for 'Who Am I?' © 1999, Celia Warren, previously unpublished; Brenda Williams for 'Harvest' and 'Apple Bobbing' © 1999, Brenda Williams, previously unpublished.

Every effort has been made to trace copyright holders and the publishers apologise for any inadvertent omissions.

British Library Cataloguing-in-Publication Data A catalogue record for this book is available from the British Library.

ISBN 0-590-53897-7

THEMES
for early years

CONTENTS

INTRODUCTION

Autumn provides an abundance of natural materials and resources just waiting to be used. Take a look out of the window to observe the many changing scenes, vivid colours and windy weather as preparations are being made for the long winter months ahead.

Children start learning about nature from babyhood, watching what is going on in the world around them as they go about their daily lives. What child can resist trampling through the fallen leaves on a windy autumn day or picking up leaves to throw high into the air or carry home?

Autumn is the season when the harvest is brought in, dried and stored to last throughout the winter. Preparations are made for the following year's growth cycle, the ground is dug and bulbs are planted for spring. The berries ripen on trees in readiness for picking and preserving. Autumn is also the time of blustery weather and fading light. It is a time of thanksgiving, a time when festivals brighten up the dark days and give us hope to get through the winter.

There are so many natural changes occurring from day to day to draw upon and the ideas in this book build upon the children's own experiences of autumn. It is packed with fascinating projects and stimulating activities based upon the popular theme of autumn. The simple clear instructions show you exactly what to do for a wide range of activities using readily available materials you can find all around you on a typical autumn day.

AIMS OF THE BOOK

Ideally, children should learn about autumn from firsthand experiences based upon their own interests. This is not always possible but their play can be enhanced and sensitively extended by providing good structured activities to complement the children's own knowledge and creativity. The aim of this book is to provide those structured activities which will enable children to discover all about the autumn season while developing skills across the curriculum.

Although not all children are able to get outdoors every day, they can watch the changing scenes of autumn through a window or make the most of even a tiny outdoor play space by taking part in these structured activities. The objective is to give the children a good, basic knowledge of the season and all that happens at this time of year. Each activity chapter focuses on a different aspect of autumn.

In Chapter 1 (Signs of autumn), children will have the chance to experience the season through firsthand observation of the weather, the wet, frosty, windy and misty mornings that go hand in hand with the season. They will take part in activities which demonstrate the richness and changing colours of the season and explore the food traditionally associated with autumn.

In Chapter 2 (Animals in autumn), children will be encouraged to find out about hedgehogs, mice and snails, they can learn about hibernation and the way animals, such as squirrels, gather food to help them survive the long winter months.

Chapter 3 (Autumn leaves) demonstrates the way some leaves fall from trees during autumn, the life cycle of leaves, their different shapes and sizes and how leaves can be used as craft materials or recycled back into the environment.

In Chapter 4 (Seeds, nuts and berries), children will discuss the important role which seeds play during the autumn season, how they scatter and their different shapes and sizes. Children will use horse chestnuts, acorns, berries and seeds for a variety of cross-curricular activities.

In Chapter 5 (Autumn games), children will have the opportunity to take part in some of the traditional games that are played during the autumn. They will look at ways in which the season can inspire games to keep them amused during the dark, misty months.

Chapter 6 (Autumn celebrations) discusses the importance of harvest, takes a look back in time at the important festivals, themes and rituals associated with autumn time and looks at the autumn traditions in some other cultures.

HOW TO USE THIS BOOK

This theme book on autumn shows children just how important and variable the season is. Many of the activities can take place outdoors, indeed learning to dress up for the autumn weather is a valuable activity in itself. There will always be children who are not happy about going outdoors in the cold, so keep a stock of suitable clothing to use outdoors and consider bringing the outdoors inside by making collections of autumn objects. If nothing else, children can view the changing seasons from a window.

When taking part in outdoor activities, it is wise to ask the children to wear wellington boots, as even on sunny days the ground remains quite wet and muddy throughout the day.

Children are never too young to care about the environment and to appreciate all the natural phenomena in the world, so what better way to start than to learn about the wonderful sights and scenes of autumn. Teach the children to look after their world as they look around them. They can learn to look after plants, trees and animals and make use of the leftover materials of the natural harvest as recycled materials for many of the activities in this book. Remind children to use only fallen leaves and twigs, to clear up after themselves, not to harm living plants and trees and to return all living creatures safely to their original habitat.

Some of the activities will require children to handle tools such as scissors, so, before beginning the activity, it is important to remind children to handle the tools with care. Encourage them to listen to instructions carefully, following each stage and only doing one thing at a time. Remind them to collect together all the resources they need before starting the activities, cover their clothes with an old shirt or apron and to roll up

their sleeves for messy activities. Always remind children to put everything away when they have finished, clean up any mess and wash their hands. Most important of all, warn children never to put any of the resources into their mouths.

When the activity is over, encourage children to share what they have done with each other by recalling what happened in a special group or discussion time. Encourage children to share the objects they have made by having a 'showing time' or setting up displays to show off their work.

Help children to get into good habits by encouraging them to plan ahead for the activity they are doing, recording and evaluating it after they have finished. It's a good idea to keep an autumn diary for this purpose, either an individual one or a group one depending on the ages and abilities of the children involved. The process does not have to be onerous; the feedback could be immediate in the form of a quick group discussion at the end of each activity.

TOPIC WEB

The Topic web is a quick, at a glance, way of seeing how the theme of autumn covers the curriculum in preparation for the National Curriculum and the Scottish 5–14 Guidelines. The Topic web can be photocopied and used as a checklist for your long-term planning.

ACTIVITY PAGES

There are six chapters in this book each covering a different aspect of autumn. Each chapter has eight activity pages which follow the same format, focusing upon a main autumn activity including two or three objectives that prepare for a National Curriculum / Scottish Guidelines subject.

The group size indicated is merely a suggestion and you can adapt the activities to suit your group's setting, its premises and the time and number of adults you have available to help carry out the activity.

The preparation for each activity is kept to a minimum. Aim to carry out the activities during autumn or just as the season is coming to a close. Sometimes the success of an activity will be based upon the assumption that children have prior experience or knowledge of certain aspects of the autumn theme. It is important to provide all the necessary experiences before such an activity takes place. Any problems can then be teased out during the introductory discussion at the start of the activity. Whenever possible, try to include the children at the planning stage.

All the equipment required is listed under the heading What you need. Involve the children in collecting all the things together and marking them off on a list before you start. You could encourage children to bring things in from home or to hunt around the setting for what they need before the activity starts. The anticipation beforehand will stimulate their interest and enthusiasm before the activity actually begins.

The What to do and Discussion sections are interdependent and should be read in conjunction with each other. They give ideas for discussion and there are simple explanations of what has happened and why. Obviously you will be talking with the children as the activity is in progress, discussing what you are doing and asking questions.

Each activity also includes a list of cross-curricular follow-up ideas for further work relating to the activity. The children will also come up with many good ideas and suggestions about what to do next themselves. The follow-up activities can be done at any time and often fit in well with other activity pages in the book.

Although the activities are grouped in chapters, they can be completed in any order and you can dip into the book to suit your group of children. Use it to supplement the good ideas already in place and to bring out the best in your children, based upon their own experiences and suggestions.

Give the children open-ended firsthand experiences and the opportunity for self-expression and originality. Do not expect them to turn out end products that are all the same.

DISPLAYS

The Display chapter includes five displays which draw together some of the ideas from different activities. Displays are a good way of recording children's work and encouraging co-operation between groups of children. They also give children the opportunity to feel pride in their work. Use carefully planned displays with clear labelling and explanations to enhance any project, making the displays interactive, useful for planning, observation, discussion, reading and enjoyment. The displays can be informative to the children and to visitors and can strengthen children's learning and improve their learning environment.

ASSEMBLIES

This chapter provides specific ideas and opportunities for sharing based upon the theme of autumn. They can be used for assemblies or group sharing times. As your group may be multicultural, extend the content of these shared experiences to include all aspects of worship. Incorporate the universal way people celebrate thanksgiving during the season of autumn, regardless of the country or climate they are in.

Each assembly has its own practical ideas on how children can be encouraged to contribute and reflect upon a specific theme, with recommendations for particular songs and prayers.

RESOURCES

This section of the book includes a useful selection of stories, songs, poems and action rhymes based on the theme of autumn. Many of them are directly referred to in the activity pages. They have been compiled to make the book self-contained and can be used in conjunction with the activity pages or on their own. All the pages in this section may be photocopied.

PHOTOCOPIABLE SHEETS

There are eight photocopiable pages in this chapter. Each one has been designed to enhance specific activities in the book. They provide a single task for the children to undertake and can be used in conjunction with the activity they refer to or alone provided the children have been given clear guidelines about how to use them.

RECOMMENDED MATERIALS

The final page in this book gives a useful list of supporting resource material, some of which has been used in conjunction with the planned activities. This includes music and songs, poems and rhymes, picture and story books, information books and other useful resources.

EXPRESSIVE ARTS

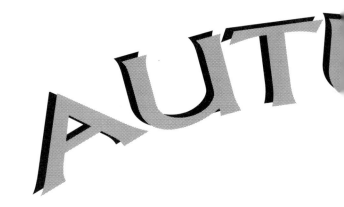

Planning towards the National Curriculum and the Scottish National guidelines 5–14

ENVIRONMENTAL STUDIES

PREPARING FOR PRIMARY SCHOOL

In England and Wales, the government has established the National Curriculum for all state schools to ensure that all children between the ages of five and sixteen cover a wide range of subjects and to ensure that any child moving to another part of the country is not disadvantaged. This means that when children enter compulsory education at five they will be covering the same areas of the curriculum for the same amount of time as a child in any other state school.

The National Curriculum subjects are English, Mathematics, Science, History, Geography, Design and Technology, Information Technology, Art, Music and PE and a locally agreed syllabus for RE. There are programmes of study in each subject area of the curriculum that give guidelines for teachers about what they should teach. There is a statutory assessment process after the children have been studying the National Curriculum for two years when they are aged approximately six or seven years old. This is based upon Standard Assessment Tasks (SATS) and the class teacher's own professional judgement.

TOWARDS LEVEL ONE

Before compulsory school, children are working towards Level One. Every child's experiences will be very different but it is essential that the curriculum they experience in the early years is child-led rather than subject based. That is to say, activities are organized for a play-based curriculum, with emphasis placed on learning through practical firsthand experiences with learning through the senses, discussion and physical activities.

This book sets out to give children a broad and balanced grounding in the subjects they will be studying in greater depth at Key Stage One.

Each activity has a learning objective that is related to a subject area of the National Curriculum but the outcomes are achieved through play. The guidelines set out in the *Desirable Outcomes for children's learning on entering compulsory education,* prescribed by the School Curriculum and Assessment Authority (now QCA) will be achieved through play in ways appropriate to the developmental stages of the children.

The Desirable Outcomes for Children's Learning are based upon six main areas – Personal and Social Development, Language and Literacy, Mathematics, Knowledge and Understanding of the World, Physical Development and Creative Development.

All the varied and imaginative play-based activities that are in this book about autumn have clear learning objectives, which link into the relevant National Curriculum subject areas but have their roots firmly in the play-based structure of the Desirable Outcomes.

THE SCOTTISH 5-14 NATIONAL GUIDELINES

In Scotland there are National Guidelines for schools concerning what should be taught to children between the ages of five and fourteen years of age.

These National Guidelines are divided into six main curriculum areas – English Language, Mathematics, Environmental Studies, Expressive Arts, Religious and Moral Education, Personal and Social Development.

These six main areas are subdivided so that 'Expressive Arts' includes art and design, drama, music and PE. All the subjects have identified strands within them; for example, Mathematics is further divided up into strands, which include problem-solving, enquiry, shape, position and movement.

The experiences offered to children in many nurseries and pre-school groups will already be laying firm foundations for this curriculum. This autumn theme book is designed in such a way that many aspects of it are covered by the activities provided, at the same time as fitting into the pre-school guidelines set out by the Scottish local education authorities.

On the Topic web on pages 8 and 9, the individual activities have been allocated to separate areas of the curriculum in order to help you organize your planning. Strands of children's Personal and Social Development are incorporated throughout the activities in this book in that the aims of this area of the early years curriculum are covered by all the activities described.

CHAPTER 1
SIGNS OF AUTUMN

Through the structured play activities in this chapter children can make patterns with fruit, observe the weather, make faces from an apple and get lost in a swirling mist! They can create their own firecracker dance, mix up autumn coloured paints, play a musical game and look at the effects of frosty weather.

FRUITY PRINTS

Objective

Mathematics – To make symmetrical patterns using fruit.

Group size

Up to six children.

What you need

An apple, a pear, an orange and a plum, a paring knife (for adult use only), sugar paper, red, yellow, orange and green ready-mixed or powder paints, four plastic trays, a plate, tissues for wiping sticky fingers.

Preparation

Cut the fruit into halves and place them on the plate ready for use. Mix the paints to a thick creamy consistency. Pour one colour into each of the plastic trays.

What to do

Let the children handle and examine the fruit. Point out patterns in the fruit. Use mathematical language to describe the shapes and patterns you can see, such as the circular shape of the orange, the triangular segments arranged symmetrically within it, the balanced seed section in the middle of the apple and the sphere-shaped plum. Point out the difference between curved and straight lines. Show the children how both sides of the fruit exactly match each other.

When the children are familiar with the properties of the fruit show them how to make fruit prints by dipping the fruit into the paint and pressing it down on the paper to create symmetrical patterns. Invite them to create their own printed patterns with the fruit. Learn 'The fruit rhyme' on page 71 of the Resources section of this book with the children, and say it as you work.

Discussion

Talk about the way the fruit ripens at the end of summer and beginning of autumn. How does the fruit look, feel and taste? Talk about the way the two halves of fruit match to make symmetrical patterns. What shapes can you see? Use mathematical language to describe the patterns. (Triangles, spheres and circles.) What time of the year does the fruit grow? What does fruit need to make it grow? (Sunlight and water.) When is it ready to pick? (End of summer / beginning of autumn.) Can you name the different parts of the fruit? (Skin, peel, flesh, pith, pip and seed.) What is your favourite piece of fruit?

Follow-up activities

✧ Take the children to an orchard or garden to see fruit growing on trees.
✧ Read the story 'Mrs Rabbit's autumn pie' on page 74.
✧ Buy some exotic fruit such as a star fruit, mango and pineapple to show the children and make some prints.
✧ Use a variety of fruit to make a fruit salad. Cut the fruit into halves and quarters to emphasize mathematical concepts of sharing.

SENSE IT'S AUTUMN

Objective

English – To describe the sounds, sights and smells of autumn.

Group size

Up to four children.

What you need

A collection of pictures, photographs and objects associated with the season of autumn, such as fir cones, horse chestnuts, dried grasses, corn, oats, wheat and barley, a sheet of sugar paper, small pieces of card, glue, scissors, a thick, felt-tipped pen and some magazine articles about autumn.

Preparation

Use the sugar paper to make a chart, writing 'Signs of autumn' at the top. Divide the rest of the space into three columns labelled 'sounds, sights and smells'. Find magazine articles about autumn. Read the poems 'Autumn bonfire' on page 72, 'When does autumn begin?' on page 67 and teach the children the song 'Signs of autumn' on page 81 as stimuli for this activity.

What to do

Show the children the autumn pictures so that they can familiarize themselves with the topic. Talk about the content of the pictures and ask the children to describe what they can see in detail.

Let them look out of the window to observe the scenes of autumn outdoors. Ask them to close their eyes to recall the sounds they might hear in autumn, these might include the wind blowing, leaves rustling as they fall from trees, conkers and acorns falling to the ground, bonfires crackling, fireworks banging or the sound of a brush as it sweeps the yard.

Make a list of all the sounds suggested on the chart. (Older children will be able to write their own lists.) Repeat the same process for the sights and smells of autumn until you have three long lists of words associated with the season of autumn.

Ask the children to cut out pictures of autumn from the magazine articles to correspond to their lists of words. Glue the pictures to the small pieces of card. (They can draw diagrams of the things they cannot find.)

When the children have a set of cards to match their lists of words, they can use them to play a matching game. Place each card face down on a flat surface. Encourage the children to take it in turns to pick up a card. Ask them to describe the scene depicted on their cards before placing them alongside the corresponding words on the chart.

Discussion

Ask the children to describe the pictures and objects. What are your favourite sounds, sights and smells of autumn? What sounds, sights and smells don't you like in autumn? What does the word autumn make you think of? How do you feel when the summer is over? What happens during autumn? What is the weather like in autumn?

Follow-up activities

✧ Make a set of feely bags or cards using dried leaves, conker shells, acorns and different dried grasses to play a guessing game.
✧ Use the same set of things to play 'Kim's game'.
✧ Suggest the children draw a picture of themselves surrounded by their favourite autumn things.
✧ Play an 'I spy' game about the sounds, sights and smells of autumn.
✧ Make some lavender bags to smell by tying lavender in a piece of net.
✧ Dry some flower petals to make pot pourri.

POMONA FACES

Objective

Art – To make a model of a face from an apple.

Group size

Four children.

What you need

A large apple for each child, a paring knife (adult use only), chopping board, cup of salt water or lemon juice, paintbrush, coloured felt-tipped pens, small offcuts of wool, florist's wire and material.

Preparation

Peel and core the apples. Cut the apples in half and brush liberally with the salt water or lemon juice to prevent them from going brown too quickly. Tell the children that they must not eat the apples.

What to do

Place the apples centre down on the chopping board. Scratch two lines across each apple half to divide it roughly into three. Make cuts about ½cm deep down the centre third of the apple to make a nose. Scoop out hollows for the eyes on each side of the nose and make two small cuts for the lips. Slice off four pieces of apple from the edges to make two ears and round off any sharp corners to make them realistic. Put the apple into a warm place to dry. Give each child a sculptured apple to use as the base for the face they are going to make.

Let the children use felt-tipped pens to mark and colour the features on their apple faces. Decorate the dried apple faces by adding bits of wool and Plasticine to complete the Pomona faces.

Discussion

Thousands of years ago the Romans held a harvest celebration each autumn in praise of Pomona, the Goddess of fruit. They thanked the Goddess Pomona for the harvest by offering her fruit and nuts. Since those times apples have always played an important part in autumn celebrations. What happens when you brush lemon juice or salt water onto the apple? (It prevents the apple from turning brown.) What happens to the apple when it is left in a warm, dry place? (It dries.) What else can you make with apples? Can you describe an apple?

Follow-up activities

✧ Make a mixed apple salad to share.
✧ Make a collection of different types of apples, label them and make a list of their names.
✧ Make a scene of different apple characters.
✧ Use an apple to touch, peel, smell, dissect and describe without saying the word 'apple'.
✧ Collect and grow some apple pips.
✧ Learn the song 'Pick! Pluck! Pull!' on page 82 of the Resources section.

MISTY MORNINGS

Objective

Science – To find out about fog and mist and to pretend to be lost in a swirling mist.

Group size

Whole group.

What you need

A safe play area and an eye mask.

What to do

Explain to the children that they are going to play a game about being lost in a swirling mist. Sit the children in a circle. Choose one child to be lost in the mist and put a mask around the child's eyes. Carefully guide the child around the inside of the circle of children, turning the masked child around a couple of times on the way. As you walk, chant the words of the traditional nursery rhyme 'One misty, moisty morning when cloudy was the weather, I chanced to meet...'. Stop at random and ask the children you stop near to introduce themselves in a funny way without saying their name, for example 'I'm a gangly girl, dressed up in green clothes. Who am I?'

When the lost child guesses the name of the stranger they swap places and the game resumes.

Repeat the game until all the children experience what it is like to be lost and unable to see in a thick swirling mist.

Discussion

Explain to the children that fog and mist are clouds that lie very close to the ground. In cities, fog combines with smoke to produce smog. Often mist appears very early in the day and burns itself off by the end of the morning. When the mist is thick it is difficult to see. What might happen when it is misty and you cannot see? (You might get lost or bump into things.) What happens when you get lost in a mist? (You cannot see familiar landmarks and tend to walk round in circles.)

Follow-up activities

✧ Read stories about foggy days such as *Postman Pat's Foggy Day* John Cunliffe (Hippo Books).
✧ Take the children outdoors on a misty day to experience walking in the mist.
✧ Invite the children to paint a picture of an autumn day. When it is dry, paint over with a white colour wash to give the effect of mist.
✧ Cut out cloud shapes from white paper. Give a cloud shape to each of the children and ask them to write a short poem about misty weather. Staple the clouds together to make a book.
✧ Read the poem 'October morning' in *A Year Full of Stories 366 Stories and Poems* Georgia Adams and Selina Young (Orion).

FIRECRACKERS

Objective

PE/Dance – To create a dance about the autumn skies.

Group size

Whole group.

What you need

A safe, clear indoor play space, a cassette player, a tape of 'Troyte' from *Enigma Variations* by Elgar or 'Sparks' from *Tommy* by The Who. Some pictures of typical bonfire night scenes.

Preparation

Show the children the pictures of bonfire scenes and discuss them. Set up the cassette player and listen to your selected piece of music to set the scene.

What to do

Explain to the children that they are going to make up a dance based upon an autumn night, when the air is full of the sights, sounds and smells of bonfires and fireworks. Choose to do this activity just after 5 November so that the children will all have some experience of such a scene.

Show the children the pictures and ask them to listen to the music to envisage the scene. Practise actions such as hop, hop, hop and jump for crackerjacks, shooting up and sinking for rockets, small sudden jumps for fire sparks, whirling round or whirling parts of body for Catherine wheels.

Begin by swaying gently to the music and build into a crescendo where the children leap skywards. Encourage them to sink gently down into different shapes at the end. Practise the dance several times to perfect it.

Discussion

Talk to the children about bonfire night. Emphasize all the safety aspects and alert them to the potential dangers of fires and fireworks. Ask the children to describe the scenes they see in the sky. Tell them to close their eyes and try to remember the sights and smells of such a night. What can you see? What happens when the sparks crackle and jump out of the fire? What happens when fireworks explode into the sky? (They light it up with lots of colours and shapes and make loud noises.) What happens to the fireworks when they have finished? (They fall to the ground and die.)

Follow-up activities

✧ Use percussion instruments to accompany the dance.

✧ Create pictures with black sugar paper and brightly coloured pastels to represent the dark sky set alight with colours.

✧ Let the children flick paint from a paintbrush onto black paper. Sprinkle with glitter to make sparkly night scenes.

✧ Read the poem 'Bonfire Night' in *A Year Full of Stories 366 Stories and Poems* Georgia Adams and Selina Young (Orion).

✧ Photocopy the 'Firecrackers' sheet on page 88 and let the children match the fireworks to the patterns they make in the sky.

AUTUMN COLOURS

Objective

Geography – To mix autumn colours to plot on an outdoor trail map.

Group size

Whole group.

What you need

Red, yellow, green, orange and brown powder paints, paint pots, brushes, palettes, white A4 paper, a safe outdoor area (preferably with some trees, bushes and other natural features).

Preparation

Prepare the materials ready for use. Take the children on a walk around your selected outdoor space, pointing out the different tones and shades of colour found in nature during the autumn. Make a basic map of the area and give a copy of it to each of the children.

What to do

Ask the children to use the powder paints to mix autumn colours. Encourage them to choose colours such as yellow, brown, orange and red to represent the colours they see around them during autumn.

Show them how to add a little black paint to make the tones darker and a little white to make them lighter.

Invite the children to mix up their own set of dark and light shades of autumn coloured paints and then to make a colour chart by painting the dark shades of paint on one side of the paper and the light shades on the other side of it.

When the colour charts are dry, take them back outdoors and retrace the route of the walk using the map. As you go, encourage the children to use their charts to match up with the colours they notice during their outdoor walk.

Back inside, decorate the maps by painting blobs of colour to correspond to the colours found in the relevant outdoor area.

Compare and contrast the natural colours found outdoors in autumn with the light and dark shades of paint on the charts.

Discussion

How do the colours change when you add the white paint? (They become lighter.) How do they change when you add the black paint? (They become darker.) How do the leaves on trees change colour during autumn? (They gradually lose their green colour as natural daylight fades. The moisture which is in them evaporates and they dry out.)

Follow-up activities

✧ Use the map at a later date to follow the trail in order to observe the way the colours of the environment change during autumn.
✧ Paint two autumn scenes which are similar. When they are dry, paint over one with a black colour wash and the other with a white colour wash. Compare the two.
✧ Make a collection of fallen leaves along the trail and mix up different shades of autumn colours to paint them.

ALL FALL DOWN

Objective

Music – To use the stimulus of autumn weather to encourage children to respond to musical signals.

Group size

Whole group.

What you need

A safe indoor play space, a tambourine, a piece of music such as Debussey's *Le vent d'ouest* or the beginning of Mars from the *Planet suite* by Holst.

Preparation

Talk to the children about the long grey days of autumn. Tell them to imagine they are outdoors in blustery, swirling winds on a wet autumn day. Set the scene by listening to the music.

What to do

Show the children the tambourine and demonstrate the sound it makes to represent the wind. Tell the children that when you stop playing, the wind dies down and it is calm. Practise running and stopping.

Play the tambourine and tell the children to move around the space as if they are being blown around by the wind. Build the music up into a crescendo with a sudden halt. Stop for a few moments. The break in the music is the signal for the children to fall down. Suggest the children whirl into place by making huge circles on the floor. Encourage the children to rise up and collapse down, turn and press down, spin quickly and stop, leap then whirl suddenly to another spot then fall down when the music stops.

Repeat these actions but ask the children to imitate the way the wind brings objects together by encouraging the children to all fall down together in a group.

Discussion

What happens when it is very wet and windy outdoors? (Branches, leaves and washing get blown around, sometimes to the ground.) What happens to objects on the ground? (They get blown around

in circles until they come to rest in a sheltered corner.) What happens to objects left outdoors in the wind and rain? (The wind blows them over or the rain washes them away.)

Follow-up activities

✧ Read the poem 'How does the wind blow?' in *A Year Full of Stories 366 Stories and Poems* Georgia Adams and Selina Young (Orion).
✧ Make wind sounds by blowing over the top of bottles filled to varying levels with water.
✧ Play Ring o' Ring o' Roses.
✧ Put a collection of heavy and light objects on a table and try to blow them over using a straw.
✧ Stir water in a jug very fast to make a whirling vortex. Watch what happens when you stop.

MR FROSTY

Objective

Science — To observe the changes that take place during frosty weather.

Group size

Up to six children.

What you need

The poem 'Jack Frost' from *The Young Puffin Book of Verse* (Puffin) — out of print, try libraries.

What to do

On a frosty day, make sure the children are dressed warmly and take them outdoors to observe the changes made overnight by the frost. Encourage the children to look closely at the world around them when it is frosty. Point out the way that branches on trees look like icy arms and fingers. Search the outdoor area looking for branches and other objects that have been frozen rigid by the frost. Ask the children to point out the features they can see.

Find a tree or bush that most resembles a person. Observe the tree periodically throughout the day and note the changes. Sometimes it will remain frozen all day long; other times the sun will melt the frost and the frosty character will disappear.

To warm up, play a game of Mr Frosty. Invite the children to run around the play space. When Mr Frosty touches them they freeze in angular shapes as if frozen stiff by the frost. Let the children take it in turns to be Mr Frosty.

Back inside ask the children to draw their own Mr Frosty character.

Discussion

Talk to the children about the way the frost transforms the outdoor environment into a white wonderland full of frozen scenes and characters. What does the frost look like? What does it remind you of? What frosty shapes or objects can you see? How does the frost feel when you touch it with your fingers? What does it sound like when you walk on it? Can you sniff the frosty air? What does it smell like? What do you think happens to the frost when it melts?

Follow-up activities

✧ Invite the children to write a poem about a character called Mr Frosty.
✧ Make frosted pictures by sprinkling sugar or silver glitter onto paper with a gluey surface.
✧ Freeze pieces of transparent plastic overnight. Scribe a figure shape onto the surface with a warm finger to make a frosty picture.
✧ Put a variety of objects outdoors on trays to freeze overnight. Next day observe the changes that have taken place.

CHAPTER 2
ANIMALS IN AUTUMN

In the autumn, all animals make preparations for the winter ahead. In this chapter, the children will learn about migration, design an animal home, look for food and search for the evidence to show that animals have been there before them. They will make cone hedgehogs, sort woodland animals into groups and snuggle up in an old blanket.

WHAT'S IN STORE?

Objective

PE/Drama – To imitate the way woodland animals move.

Group size

Whole group.

What you need

A safe, indoor space with room to move freely.

Preparation

Set the scene by explaining to the children that they are going to be little woodland animals. In autumn, the animals venture out from the safety of their homes to forage for food in order to build up food stores to see them through the winter hibernation period. (See Discussion.)

What to do

Let the children practise moving like a variety of woodland animals before they choose their favourite one. Suggest a few ideas to start them off:
• The field mouse could scuttle along on all fours, stopping and darting for cover when anything moves.
• The squirrel could run out, turn and quickly dart back for cover.
• The rabbit could hop about, stopping to prick up his ears before returning to the search. If anything moves the rabbit will freeze on the spot.
   Invite the children to create a variety of movements to represent different woodland animals. Ask the children to choose their favourite animal and gradually build up a story in movement about the way little animals collect and make food stores ready for winter. Let them finish by moving back to a place of hibernation, and lie on the floor in a sleeping position. Practise the movement several times until all the children are competent.

Discussion

Explain that some animals survive during the winter months when food is scarce by sleeping for long periods of time. This is called hibernation. Tell them that the cool nights and shortage of food in autumn is the sign for some animals to become less active in readiness for hibernation. During early autumn, some animals such as squirrels and badgers build little nests with food stores to see them through the long winter months.
   Explain that, during hibernation, animals often wake for food and to build new nests. What do some animals do in autumn? (Prepare food stores.) Why do some animals hibernate? (Food is scarce and it is cold.) How do field mice move? (They scuttle around.) How does a rabbit/hedgehog/squirrel move?

Follow-up activities

✧ Learn the counting rhyme 'Squirrel store' on page 68 so that the children can chant it as they play.
✧ Make a collection of things people might need if they hibernated like woodland animals.
✧ Tell the story of *The Town Mouse and the Country Mouse* (Traditional).
✧ Look for information about woodland animals in reference books.
✧ Photocopy the sheet 'Food for squirrel' on page 89. Ask the children to colour in the trees and cut out the acorn shapes. Match the correct number of acorns to the trees.

FLY AWAY

Objective

Geography – To play a game based on the way some birds fly south in autumn.

Group size

Whole group.

What you need

A safe outdoor play area and some chalk.

Preparation

Draw two lines with chalk to represent north and south. Read the poem 'Flying away' on page 68 of the Resources section. Encourage the children to pretend that their hands are birds flying.

What to do

Explain to the children that some birds migrate when the weather gets colder. (See Discussion.) Take the children outdoors and show them the chalk markings, tell them that one line represents the north and the other the south. Explain that all the birds are in the north until the autumn when they get ready to fly south for the winter.

Invite the children to stand behind the line that indicates the north and encourage them to pretend to be birds looking for food. Say that, on the signal of a clap, the autumn wind blows up and they have to 'fly' off to the chalk line representing the south.

Extend the game by chalking other features on the ground. Use blue chalk lines to represent the seas and yellow chalk lines to represent the desert. An adult could chase the children, pretending to be the wind blowing behind them. If the 'wind' touches them when they are between the blue lines they have to pretend to swim across the sea to the south. If the 'wind' touches them when they are between the yellow lines they have to pretend to trek across the desert to the south line. When they are touched they are out of the game. The last 'bird' left in the game is 'the wind' next time. Everyone returns to the north and the migration process starts over again.

Discussion

In autumn some birds such as swallows and starlings fly south in search of a warm climate and to find food. In the spring, they fly back home to the north to build their nests. This journey is called migration. They prepare for the long flight by eating a lot during early autumn to build up fat stores beneath their wings. The birds fly over dangerous deserts and seas without stopping. Where do birds fly in autumn? (South.) Why do birds fly south in autumn? (To look for warmth and food.) How can you help the birds that stay? (Feed them.) What do the birds do when they get back home? (Build nests.)

Follow-up activities

✧ Learn the song 'Time to say goodbye' on page 84 of the Resources section of this book.
✧ Watch flocks of birds in early autumn when they fly south.
✧ Make some bobbing birds from clothes pegs, scraps of paper and material.
✧ Learn the rhymes 'Two Little Dicky-birds Sitting On a Wall' and 'Five Little Sparrows I Can See' from *This Little Puffin* Elizabeth Matterson (Puffin).
✧ Use the photocopiable sheet 'Make a bird kite' on page 90 to make a fly-away bird. Glue the bird shape to a piece of thin card and cut around the outline. Fold the bird shape in half along the broken line a–b. Fold the wings outwards along the broken lines c–d. Fold the head inwards to make the shape of a bird c–e. Cut a small hole at point x and attach a piece of wool or string.

HOME TO HIBERNATE

Objective

Design and Technology — To design and make a home for a small woodland animal to hibernate.

Group size

Four children.

What you need

A variety of cardboard boxes (shoe boxes or cereal boxes), some scraps of paper, corrugated cardboard, a variety of materials such as offcuts of corduroy, velvet, cotton wool, fur fabric, natural materials such as straw, twigs leaves, feathers, pipe-cleaners, elastic bands, florists wire, paper clips, staples, staple gun, scissors, glue.

Preparation

Introduce the activity by talking about the way some animals build nests in autumn as part of their preparations for the long cold months ahead. Explain that they go out in search of bits and pieces in order to make their nests warm and comfortable.

Point out to the children that some animals like foxes, rabbits and badgers build their homes underground, while others build their homes in hedgerows, bushes or trees.

What to do

Ask the children to imagine that they are little woodland creatures who hibernate during the long cold months of winter. Invite the children to choose a cardboard box to use as a base for their nest or home. Let them use the scrap materials to turn the box into a comfortable place to spend the winter. Present them with a variety of natural and manufactured materials.

Encourage the children to think about suitable materials they could use and ways of joining them to the box to make the home secure. Ask them to line the box with materials that are cosy and will keep the animal warm. Suggest that they find different ways of attaching the materials to the box using elastic bands, paper fasteners, pipe-cleaners, florist wire, glue and staples. Make sure that there are no rough ends and that the joining materials

stay safely in place. When the inside of the box is complete, invite the children to choose materials to cover it so that it is camouflaged. Put all the boxes on display together to make a woodland scene full of hidden homes.

Discussion

Talk about the children's own homes. Where do you live? What is your home like? (Comfortable, cosy.) What little creature are you going to make a home for? Does your animal live underground or above the ground? Does it live in a nest, a burrow, hole in a tree or under the bushes? What can you find outdoors to make the home comfortable? (Small pieces of straw, hair, feathers, leaves and dried grass.) What else could you put in your home to help you see the winter through? (A food store.) Why does the home have to be camouflaged? (So that the animal inside it can safely hibernate without being disturbed.)

Follow-up activities

✧ Make a little animal to live in the home using pipe-cleaners and scraps of natural materials.
✧ Make an underground/overground display showing where animals build their nests in autumn. (See page 61 in the Displays section.)
✧ Go outdoors to look for evidence of animals' homes, but be careful not to disturb them.
✧ Use the 'Finger mouse puppet' template on page 91 to make a finger mouse to live in the home.

TAME THE MOUSE

Objective

PE – To play a game of taming the wild mouse.

Group size

Four to ten children.

What you need

A safe, flat outdoor play space, chalk.

Preparation

Draw a large chalk circle measuring 10 metres in diameter on the ground where the game is going to take place. Check the area to ensure there are no safety hazards.

What to do

Go outdoors into the play area where you have marked out the circle. Explain the boundaries of the game to the children. Talk to them about safety issues and tell them to take care not to bump into each other while they are playing the game.

Choose one player to stand inside the circle and explain that this child is the tame mouse guarding the food stored for winter. All the other children stand outside the circle pretending to be wild mice. The wild mice venture inside the circle foraging for food. They tease the tame mouse by creeping up to the circle and putting one foot inside it, or by quickly scuttling across the circle trying not to get caught. If the 'tame mouse' touches one of the 'wild' ones while they have even one foot inside the circle, that wild mouse also becomes tame. The new tame mouse stays in the circle and helps the first tame mouse to catch the rest. The last wild mouse to be caught plays the tame one in the next game.

Discussion

During autumn, some animals look for food to store for the long cold winter months. The animals that hibernate will be eating all the food they can find during the autumn to build up the fat in their bodies. Other animals such as squirrels and mice will be foraging around in the undergrowth gathering food to store away in their homes, to help them survive the difficult winter months when there is very little food to be found. Where do mice search for food? (In the undergrowth and hedgerows.) What kind of food do mice eat? (Nuts and berries.) Where do mice put all the food they find? (Mice store food in their nests.) How do mice move? (They quietly scuttle along.) How do mice eat? (They nibble.) Why do mice have big ears? (To hear well to help them avoid danger.) Why are mice covered in fur? (To keep warm as they live outdoors.) Discuss the differences between tame and wild mice. For example, a wild mouse has to search for food whereas a tame mouse is feed by its owner.

Follow-up activities

✧ Invite an owner of a pet mouse to bring the mouse to visit the group. Observe the behaviour of the mouse.
✧ Read stories about mice such as *Happy Mouseday* Dick King-Smith (Corgi Pups).
✧ Draw a large picture of a mouse and play 'Pin the Tail on the Mouse'.
✧ Make a collection of toy mice.
✧ Use the photocopiable template on page 91 to make a finger mouse.

WHO'S BEEN HERE?

Objective

History – To look for signs that animals leave behind them.

Group size

Whole group.

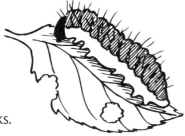

What you need

A leaf with bite marks.

Preparation

Begin by telling the children that autumn is the best time to look for signs of little creatures. Tell them that some animals such as snails leave trails behind them. Explain that insects are abundant in autumn but like all other animals, they face the problem of surviving the cold winter. Autumn is the season when they are out and about making preparations for winter. Autumn is the time to look for big, fully-grown, juicy caterpillars about to turn into chrysalises. Show them the leaves, which have been partly eaten. Invite them to examine the leaves closely.

What to do

Take the children outdoors on a dry autumn day. Explain that they are going on a minibeast hunt. Tell them to look on leaves for signs, such as bite marks where caterpillars or snails have been to eat. Tell the children to look around them carefully to discover some surprises of nature for themselves.

Invite them to look under stones for signs of snail's silvery trails and under rotting logs for woodlice, spiders or beetles. Ensure that they replace all objects and return the creatures they find to their natural habitat.

Discussion

Tell the children that if they look closely all around them, they will be able to see the signs that insects leave behind them such as trails, footprints or bite marks. Have you ever seen little round eggs on the underside of a leaf? What signs do snails leave behind them? (Silvery trail marks.) What signs do woodlice leave behind them? (Powdery wood where they have eaten through it.) How do you know when a caterpillar has eaten a leaf? (There are little round holes in it.) How does a caterpillar move? (Crawls along slowly.)

Follow-up activities

✧ Examine a leaf with bite marks on it under a microscope or with a magnifying glass.
✧ Read *The Very Hungry Caterpillar* Eric Carle (Hamish Hamilton).
✧ Make a caterpillar from an egg box.
✧ Dip a marble in silver paint and roll it around on some black paper to make snail trails.
✧ Make spirals by cutting a circle like the pattern on a snail's shell. Look for other spiral shapes.
✧ Stuff an old sock with newspaper and tie the end. Decorate it with string and bits of material to make a caterpillar puppet.
✧ Carefully put a snail on a piece of black sugar paper to watch it making a trail. (Ensure that afterwards you return the snail to the place where you found it.)

CRAFTY CONES

Objective

Art – To make a hedgehog from a fir cone.

Group size

Up to four children.

What you need

Some large fir cones, glue, sunflower seeds, string, scraps of felt or paper, grey, white and brown ready-mixed or powder paints and paintbrushes.

Preparation

Collect together all the necessary materials and make a hedgehog from one of the fir cones as an example to show the children.

What to do

Show the children the sample hedgehog and explain how you made it. Encourage them to use the materials provided to make their own model hedgehogs. Remind the children not to eat any of the seeds.

Ask them to find ways of attaching the seeds and pieces of material they have chosen for the animal's features to the cones. Encourage the children to find ways of making their hedgehogs realistic and original. Can they find a way to make their hedgehogs stand up on their feet? Let them try making a variety of different poses. Some could be made as if they are rolled up into a ball, others could be sleeping, eating or standing up on their back legs.

When the glue is dry, ask the children to paint their hedgehogs to make them look realistic.

Discussion

Talk to the children about hedgehogs. Explain that during the autumn a hedgehog becomes less active before settling down to hibernate for the winter. Tell them that the hedgehog has a spiny coat and it sniffs around in the hedgerows during autumn. Have you ever seen a hedgehog? Can you describe it? Why does a hedgehog have so many spines? (To protect it.) What does a hedgehog do in winter? (It hibernates.) What noise does a hedgehog make? (It snuffles.) Tell the children that pine and fir trees are called conifers. Conifers produce cones that carry seeds. How can you tell the difference between pine and fir trees? (Fir trees have short needles and long thin cones. Pine trees have long needles and round cones.) How can you tell the weather by a pine cone? (When dry weather is coming the cones open up.)

Follow-up activities

✧ Say the rhyme 'One little hedgehog' on page 69 of the Resources section and learn the actions to go with it.
✧ Use playdough or clay to make a hedgehog's body. Press straws, lolly sticks or pipe-cleaners into the body to make a spiny coat.
✧ Compile a book about hedgehogs by asking the children to write or draw all they know about them. Mount each child's work on to a hedgehog-shaped silhouette and staple the pages together to make a book.
✧ Use cones, teasels and thistles to make a collection of small woodland animals such as mice and owls. Display them in a woodland scene.
✧ Put one cone in a dry warm place and another in a damp place. Leave them for a few days to see what happens.

WHO AM I?

Objective

Mathematics – To make woodland animal cards to sort into sets.

Group size

Four children.

What you need

Pencil, sheets of thin A4 card, scissors, glue, coloured felt-tipped pens or scraps of materials such as wool, feathers and hessian.

Preparation

Photocopy the sheet 'Autumn animals' on page 92 onto card to provide one for each child.

What to do

Hand out the photocopiable sheet to each child. Cut out the cards so that each child has a complete set of animals. Encourage the children to colour the cards or glue on pieces of scrap materials to make the animals look realistic. (Remind the children to keep the cards as flat as possible so that they can be used in a card game later on.) String, seeds and scraps of leather are useful to use as feet, tails, eyes and noses. When the cards are finished, leave them to dry.

Shuffle the cards and place them, picture side down, on a flat surface. Invite the children to pick them up in turn to sort the pictures into sets – let the children decide the criteria for sorting the cards. They could be sorted into the same species, animals with or without tails, animal that hibernate in winter, animals that live underground or animals that fly or do not fly.

Discussion

Talk about the woodland animals you might see during autumn. Discuss their similarities and differences. Ask the children to tell you all they know about woodland animals and if they have seen any of them. Why do you think woodland animals forage around in hedgerows in autumn? (They are looking for food.)

Follow-up activities

✧ Encourage the children to make a nature book and record all the woodland animals they see during autumn.
✧ Hide the cards under objects and challenge the children to find them.
✧ Make models of woodland animals using corks, scraps of material and wool.
✧ Make sets of the animals in three different sizes to sort according to families.
✧ Use the cards to make a lift-the-flap tree showing where the animals live.
✧ Read the story *The Owl's Lesson* Nick Butterworth (Harper Collins).
✧ Read and learn the number rhymes 'Ten Little Squirrels sat on a Tree' and 'Five Little Mice Came Out to Play' from *This Little Puffin* Elizabeth Matterson (Puffin).

BLANKET HOME

Objective

English — To build up vocabulary through play.

Group size

Up to six children.

What you need

A safe area in which children can move around freely, one blanket for each child taking part.

Preparation

Place the blankets in separate heaps around the play area.

What to do

Tell the children that woodland animals live in a place that is warm in summer and cold in winter. During autumn, the woodland animals are out searching for somewhere to make their home for the winter.

Invite the children to be little woodland animals foraging around the space until they find a blanket. Tell the children to use the blanket to make themselves a snug nest in which to spend the winter. When they are wrapped up in their nests, tell them to pretend to go to sleep.

While they are sleeping, encourage them to think of words to describe the way they feel inside their little homes. After a while, someone clearing out the hedgerow or cutting down the trees disturbs them. Tell the children to quickly pick up their blanket and run off in search of a new place to make a home.

Repeat these actions several times. Ask the children to repeat the activity with a partner, using two blankets to share a nest. Then encourage the whole group to work together to make a home with all the blankets. After the activity, invite the children to make a list of all the words they could use to describe the way they felt, when they were snuggled up inside their blanket and then when they were disturbed. Older children could scribe for themselves.

Discussion

Talk to the children about the way some woodland animals spend autumn preparing their nests for winter. Explain that when they are disturbed they move on to make a new home. What would you use to make a nest if you lived in the woods? (Twigs, leaves, feathers and bits of hair.) How would you feel if you were disturbed when you were hibernating? (Cross.) What did you feel like when you were snuggled up inside your blanket? (Warm and cosy.) How do you feel when you snuggle up in bed at home? (Safe and warm.)

Follow-up activities

✧ Use the list of words to make up a poem about setting up a home or making a nest in autumn.
✧ Make a pictogram by drawing a diagram to match each word.
✧ Use simple reference books to find out how animals prepare for winter during the autumn and take it in turns to report back findings to the group.
✧ Practise making your bed at home.

CHAPTER 3
AUTUMN LEAVES

The changing colours of autumn leaves provides the activities for this chapter with ideas to make skeleton leaves, create a collage, make leaf prints, dance like leaves falling from trees and design some creeping foliage to decorate a room.

LEAF SKELETON

Objective

Science – To make a skeleton leaf.

Group size

Up to six children.

What you need

Hard, shiny leaves, rainwater, a plastic bowl, clear glue and a sheet of white paper.

Preparation

Collect a few hard, shiny leaves (horse chestnut, laurel or aspen). Put half of them into a bowl of rainwater and leave them outside for several weeks. Don't change the rainwater.

What to do

Bring the bowl of leaves inside. Show the children the dry leaves and the leaves in the bowl of rainwater. Put the dry leaves to one side. Pour off the rainwater and pick out the wet leaves. Show the children how to scrape the remaining fleshy part of the leaf with their fingers. Rinse the leaf gently under a tap and you should be left with the skeleton. Pat the skeleton leaf dry with a piece of kitchen roll and show it to the children. Invite them to carefully handle it to familiarize themselves with its properties.

Compare the skeleton leaves with the dry, green ones and encourage the children to compare them. Give each child one of the leaves that has been soaking in water together with a piece of kitchen roll. Challenge the children to carefully pick out the fleshy bits to make their own skeleton leaf.

Mount the leaves on white paper with little blobs of clear glue. Make enough skeletons to make patterns.

Discussion

Talk about the different types of leaf. Explain that some leaves are stronger than others and that some make better skeletons. Point out the different parts of a leaf such as the veins and flesh. Explain that leaves fall from trees in autumn and dry out. They gradually rot to leave a skeleton of veins. What did the skeleton leaf look like before it was soaked in rainwater? (Green and shiny.) Why do the leaves in the rainwater smell? (They have gone stale and rotten.) What do the leaves look like after they have been soaked in the rainwater? (Brown and soggy.)

Follow-up activities

✧ Search for skeleton leaves under shrubs. Make a collection of them and try to identify the skeletons.

✧ Press waxy leaves between layers of white paper. Mount the pressed leaves in a book to make an identification guide. Use the white paper to make leaf pictures by colour washing over the waxy marks left by the leaf as it dries out.

✧ Sort the leaves by different criteria – large/small, thick/thin, smooth edge/crinkled edge, lots of veins/few veins, lots of colour/few colours, whole/broken, single/compound.

✧ Examine a leaf under a microscope to discover the network of veins.

✧ Play 'Pass the Leaf' – pass a leaf around a group of children sitting in a circle. Ask them to say one word to describe the leaf before passing it on.

A LEAFY FACE

Objective

Art – To make a collage of a face with leaves.

Group size

Up to six children.

What you need

Six papers plates, an assortment of fallen leaves in different colours, shapes and sizes and some glue.

Preparation

Collect some fallen leaves and dry them out by laying them between two sheets of newspaper. Put heavy books on top and leave for about two weeks. The leaves will be flat and dry ready for use. Make up an example of a face using the materials.

What to do

Show the children the sample face you have already made. Give them each a plate, an assortment of leaves and some glue and invite them to arrange the leaves on the paper plate in the shape of a face. When they are happy with their design tell them to glue the leaves into position. Leave the finished design to dry. Tie the plates to string and hang them up so that they blow in the wind like mobiles.

Alternatively, attach the plates to branches or sticks using sticky tape and string and display them in scenes of autumn leaves and trees.

Discussion

What did the leaves feel like when you were arranging them into place? (Dry and papery.) Why were some leaves easier to stick to the paper than others were? (The waxy leaves were slippery to handle.) How did you manage to keep the leaves in place when you were making your leaf face? Sometimes the shapes of leaves and trees remind you of other things. Can you think of any shapes or objects made by branches and trees that you have? (Perhaps a bush in the shape of a cat, or a tree that looks like the outline of an old man.)

Follow-up activities

✧ Make leaf masks using paper plates – cut out holes for the eyes and tie in place pieces of wool or string.
✧ Make other leaf pictures to resemble realistic objects.
✧ Scrunch up different coloured leaves to make leaf mosaic plates. Varnish the leaves to preserve them.
✧ Go outdoors on a dry day to look up at the leaves on a tree to see if you can spot any faces. Do the same with clouds.
✧ Learn the song 'Mister Autumn' on page 80 in the Resources section.

THEMES
for early years

LEAF PRINTS

Objective

English — To identify leaf prints.

Group size

Up to six children.

What you need

A variety of fallen leaves, white A4 paper, two sheets of newspaper, some brown, reddish and tan boot polish, kitchen roll, aprons.

Preparation

Collect some fallen leaves. Look around to find out which trees they have come from. Place the leaves between two sheets of newspaper and leave them to dry out. Ask the children to put aprons on.

What to do

When the leaves are flat and dry, gently smear the lower surface with polish, using some kitchen roll or a finger. Spread the polish evenly and sparingly. Place the leaf (polish side down) on a sheet of white paper. Cover it with another sheet of white paper. Gently rub on the top sheet of paper with your fingers. Lift the top piece of paper to reveal a coloured print of the leaf.

When the children have finished making leaf prints, ask them to wash their hands. Use reference books to classify the leaves according to species.

Label them together — older children can do this for themselves.

Discussion

Explain to the children that prints make interesting and effective records of their leaf collections. Encourage them to focus their attention on the leaf form, plant structure and to observe the patterns they make. Ask them to identify the names of the trees the leaves came from. Which leaves are small? Which are large? Which leaves are simple shapes? Which leaves are made up of many leaflets? Which leaves have lots of veins? Which have few? Which leaves are smooth to touch? Which are rough and wrinkled? Which leaves have smooth edges? Which leaves have serrated edges?

Follow-up activities

✧ Make prints in the same way using poster paints.
✧ Make prints of leaves using carbon paper instead of boot polish.
✧ Make scatter prints. Place a leaf on a sheet of white paper, run your fingers over the bristles of a paint-covered brush to flick the paint and then remove the leaf to reveal the white silhouette.
✧ Make scribble prints. Put the leaf on newspaper (lower surface up), cover with white paper and rub with a crayon or a pencil. Cut out the leaf shape and mount onto coloured paper or card.
✧ Make a simple reference book by stapling several pages of leaf prints together.
✧ Press leaves into clay or playdough. Cut around the leaves and dry. Challenge the children to match the real leaves to the ones they have made.

SHADES OF AUTUMN

Objective

History – To note the effects of the passage of time on leaves.

Group size

Up to six children.

What you need

Clipboards, sheets of white A4 paper, access to a tree with low-hanging branches, six pieces of different coloured wool and ready-mixed or powder paints in autumn shades.

Preparation

Find a deciduous tree with a low-hanging branch. Attach the paper to the clipboards.

What to do

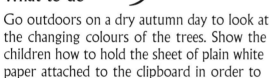

Go outdoors on a dry autumn day to look at the changing colours of the trees. Show the children how to hold the sheet of plain white paper attached to the clipboard in order to trace a leaf growing on the tree.

Invite the children to make several traces of the leaf on their paper, encouraging them to take care not to damage the tree or pull the leaf from the branch. Give each child a piece of wool and tell them to mark their chosen leaf by gently tying the piece of wool around its stalk.

Back inside, ask the children to colour one of their leaf outlines to match the colours in the leaf. Watch the leaf each day during autumn. Make a pictogram by repeating the activity several times throughout the season. Ask the children to compare and contrast the difference between their coloured leaf outlines.

Discussion

Explain to the children that some trees are deciduous – they lose their leaves in autumn. They do this because their leaves cannot work properly in cold weather and there is not enough sunlight in autumn for the leaves to make food for the tree. Some leaves, such as holly, have a waxy coating which helps them survive the winter. Explain that the leaf's upper surface is often glossy to stop the sun from drying out the leaf. Point out that leaves change colour before they fall. As a leaf dies, the fleshy part dries out causing a change in colour. Trees of the same species go through the same pattern of colour changes, although each tree changes colour at its own rate. What happens to some leaves in autumn? (The leaves change colour.) Why do the leaves change colour? (They dry out and the colours in them fade.)

Follow-up activities

✧ Learn the song 'Colour me autumn' page 83 in the resources section.
✧ Older children could make a written record of the changing colours of leaves in autumn.
✧ Watch the marked leaf from day-to-day to track how long it takes for the green leaf to change colour and fall from the tree.
✧ Make pictogram records for a variety of deciduous trees to contrast the results.
✧ Find out if leaves give off water. Tie a plastic bag over the end of a leafy twig, leave it overnight and see how much water collects inside the bag.

BRANCHING OUT

• •

Objective

Art — To make a collage of an autumn tree.

Group size

Up to four children.

What you need

Strong thin paper, masking tape, wax crayons, a selection of fallen leaves, two sheets of newspaper, a pile of heavy books, scissors, glue and some blue sugar paper.

Preparation

Tape some thin paper to a tree trunk with the masking tape. Choose a youngish bark, free from moss or lichen that shows a characteristic pattern. (Oak has widely spaced ridges, lime has diamond shapes, and holly makes little dots and dashes all over the rubbing.) Dry some leaves between two sheets of newspaper under a pile of heavy books.

What to do

Take the children outdoors to look at trees. Look at all the different tree shapes and point out the way each tree has its own typical shape which depends on the arrangement of branches. Make

quick sketches of tree shapes to use as a plan for the tree collage.

Take the children to the tree where you have taped the white drawing paper. Demonstrate how to make a bark rubbing. Rub over the white paper using the side of a wax crayon until a pattern appears. Invite the children to make their own bark rubbing. Take the rubbing down from the tree trunk. Back indoors cut out a trunk from the bark rubbing. Glue it onto the blue sugar paper and glue the dried leaves onto the top of the trunk to make a collage of a tree in autumn.

Discussion

Discuss the different parts of a tree to encourage an appreciation of its structure. Encourage careful observation of the tree, focusing on its form. What does the tree look like in autumn? Explain that the outside of the tree trunk is covered in a hard, tough layer of bark. The bark protects the tree from drying out and from damage by insects or animals. When the tree is young, the bark is thin and smooth but as it gets older, it thickens to form different patterns. Tell the children that you can identify the tree by its bark. What texture is the bark of the tree? (Rough.) What do the leaves feel like when they are dry? (Papery.) Is the tree large or small? What is happening to the leaves? (They are turning brown and falling off.) What does the trunk look like? (Tall and round.)

Follow-up activities

✧ Make a leaf rubbing using the same technique.
✧ Make a collage of the tree using leaf prints instead of real ones.
✧ Make several 'trees' to create an autumn woodland scene.
✧ Make bark rubbings of different trees to compare and contrast the patterns of their bark.
✧ Make rubbings using tinted paper, typing paper, tracing paper or greaseproof paper to achieve different results.
✧ Do a tree census by making a simple map of the area studied. Mark in the main features and plot the trees you study. Record the findings on a simple census chart.
✧ Learn the action rhyme 'Here are the trees' on page 70 of the Resources section.
✧ Read the book *Tattybogle* Sandra Horn and Ken Brown (Hodder).

SORTED LEAF SHAPES

Objective

Mathematics – To collect leaves to sort into sets.

Group size

Whole group.

What you need

A safe outdoor area, paper bags, several different species of fallen leaves, a flat surface to work on, a piece of sugar paper and some glue.

Preparation

Dress the children up warmly and give them a paper bag each to put their leaves in.

What to do

Choose a dry autumn day and take the children outdoors for a walk to collect fallen leaves. Back indoors, ask the children to place their leaves on a flat surface ready for sorting.

Challenge the children to sort the leaves into different sets. They could sort them according to their shape, into piles of large or small leaves, into groups of thick or thin ones, into groups of smooth-edged or crinkle-edged leaves and into leaves that have lots of veins or a few veins. They could group the leaves into ones that are made up of several different shades or colours or into leaves of one colour and into piles of green or brown ones. They could sort the leaves into whole or broken ones or group them according to whether they are single or compound leaves (many leaflets). Let the children decide the criteria for sorting the leaves themselves.

When the children have sorted the leaves, ask them to glue them into sets onto the sugar paper. Leave them to dry. Label the leaves according to the criteria in which they were sorted, in order to compare and contrast their different properties.

Discussion

Talk about the leaves as the children handle them. How are the leaves arranged on the twig? (They can be opposite each other in pairs, or they can be single and alternate from one side of the twig to the other.) Ask the children to look at the colour and surface of the different leaves. Encourage them to describe what they feel and see when they are sorting the leaves. Explain that leaves in one piece are called single, while those made up of many leaflets are called compound. What are the differences between the leaves? (Some are different shapes, colours and sizes.) How many different sorts of leaves have you found?

Follow-up activities

✧ Glue the leaves to a piece of paper to record the findings. Make a leaf scrapbook by mounting the leaves into a notebook. Label the leaves and write down where and when you found them.
✧ Scrunch up the different leaves to make leaf mulch for the garden.
✧ Make an attractive collage of an autumn scene with the leaves.
✧ Identify the leaves by matching them to the pictures in simple reference books.
✧ Make a compost heap with the leaves or use as mulch to keep plants warm in winter.
✧ Find ways of making evenly-spaced crunching sounds when walking on dry leaves and chant the rhyme 'Autumn carpet' on page 69 as you walk along.
✧ Read the book *Out and about* Shirley Hughes (Walker Books).

TUMBLING LEAVES

Objective

PE/Dance – To imitate the movement of leaves falling from a tree.

Group size

Whole group.

What you need

A space which is large enough for all the children to move around in safely.

Preparation

Take the children outdoors on a sunny autumn day when leaves are falling from the trees. Invite them to stand under the tree to fully experience the falling of the autumn leaves. Tell them to look up at the tree canopy.

What to do

Remind the children how the autumn leaves fall from the trees. Talk about the way the wind can blow them off so they tumble down together. Explain that they are going to pretend to be the autumn leaves tumbling down from the trees.

Ask the children to stretch up towards the sky as far as they can. On the signal of a clap, challenge them to fall to the floor as if they are leaves being blown from a tree. When they are near the floor, ask the children to lie still in an interesting shape. After a while, the wind blows up again. Encourage the children to roll over the floor like leaves swirling around in the wind.

Discussion

Talk to the children about the way the tree canopy decreases in autumn as leaves fall from the trees. What can you see when you look up into the canopy? (Leaves, patterns of light and shade, different colours and leaves coming down.) How does it feel to stand under a tree when the leaves are tumbling down? What can you hear as leaves fall to the ground? (Rustling noises.) What happens to the leaves when they fall down? (They get blown around, trodden on, eaten by animals, they dry out and rot and they return to the soil to make it fertile.) Have you ever walked through a pile of dried leaves? What sounds did you hear? (Crunching and cracking.)

Follow-up activities

✧ Read the story 'Falling leaves' on page 76 in the Resources section of this book.
✧ Go back to the tree when it has shed all its leaves. Stand under it and look at the canopy again. Compare what you can see with your first visit.
✧ Go for a walk through fallen leaves when it is windy. Discuss the experience.
✧ Monitor a deciduous tree from the beginning to the end of autumn. Record what it looks like on a chart.

CREEPING FOLIAGE

Objective

Design and Technology – To join paper leaves to string to make foliage.

Group size

Four children.

What you need

Three metres of sisal rope, pipe-cleaners, thick, green paper, sticky tape, pencil and scissors.

Preparation

Take the children outdoors to show them the way creeper plants, such as ivy, wind themselves around trees. Gather all the materials together and make up a sample of the creeping foliage to show the children the basic idea.

What to do

Give each child a sheet of green paper and ask them to fold it into rectangles about 15 × 20cm. Invite them to draw a typical leaf shape on the upper layer of the paper. Help them to cut out the leaves through all the layers of paper. When all the leaves have been cut out, encourage the children to draw leaf designs on each leaf to give them a realistic appearance.

Ask the children to lay a pipe-cleaner down the centre of the underside of the leaf and fix it in place with sticky tape or glue to make the stem. Encourage them to twist the pipe-cleaner stalks around the rope until there are enough leaves along it to make a long creeper.

To make the leaves look more realistic, encourage the children to bend them into curved shapes. Use the creeping plant to decorate a room or a den, or as the border for an autumn display.

Discussion

Talk about the way that some foliage, such as ivy, winds itself around other trees. Have you ever seen any creeper plants? Where do creeper plants grow? (Under the hedgerows around the bottoms of trees and up their trunks.) What does a creeper plant look like? (It has a long winding stem with lots of leaves either side of it.)

Follow-up activities

✧ Make a potted plant with the pipe-cleaner leaves. Paint a cardboard tube brown, leave it to dry and add trunk markings. Push a ball of Plasticine into the top of the tube and push the wire stalks of the leaves down into the Plasticine, then bend them into shape. Stand the plant in a flowerpot full of sand.

✧ Make plants in autumn shades to display as a garden scene with the creeping foliage.

✧ Create an autumn den making up several strands of the creeping foliage to cover a small play area.

✧ Use the foliage as scenery for a play about autumn.

✧ Play the game 'Follow My Leader' through fallen leaves.

✧ Learn the song 'Five Little Leaves So Bright and Gay' in *This Little Puffin* compiled by Elizabeth Matterson (Puffin).

✧ Photocopy the sheet 'Colourful leaves' on page 93 and use a dice to play the creeping foliage game. Make a colour dice with the colours red, brown, green and yellow and leaving two sides blank. Throw the dice in turn, if you land on a colour move your counter to the next leaf of that colour. If you throw a blank, miss a turn and pass the dice on.

CHAPTER 4
SEEDS, NUTS AND BERRIES

Use the natural harvest of autumn as stimulus for structured activities. Children can make a seed collage, discover how seeds disperse, find out if seeds are dead or alive, sort nuts into sets, design a pendant to wear, use berry juice to tie-dye cloth and create a dance about scattering seeds.

HIDDEN SEEDS

Objective

Art – To make a seed collage.

Group size

Four children.

What you need

A pumpkin, a paring knife (adult use only), absorbent kitchen paper, a variety of flat seeds (ash, sycamore, elm, pumpkin, sunflower), a sheet of stiff paper or card and glue.

Preparation

Show the children a pumpkin, let them handle it and discuss what it feels and looks like. Whenever you use seeds, nuts or berries for an activity remind the children not to eat them. Cut the pumpkin into quarters and give a piece to each child to observe in detail. Encourage them to scoop out the seeds with their fingers and then wash their hands. Wash the seeds and put them aside to dry.

What to do

Give each child a sheet of paper, some glue and a variety of flat seeds. Encourage the children to examine and handle the seeds to familiarize themselves with their properties, then invite them to sort the seeds into similar shapes and sizes. Explain that they are going to use the seeds to make a colourful autumn collage.

Suggest a couple of simple ideas, depending on the children's interests at the time, and encourage them to arrange the seeds into a pleasing pattern. When the children are satisfied with their designs, invite them to stick their seeds onto the paper to create a seed collage.

Discussion

Fruits containing seeds grow from flowers. The seeds inside the fruit ripen in autumn. In order to grow, the seeds need to find their way to the ground, where there is food and light. Seeds are dispersed in different ways. How do seeds find their way to the ground? (Birds, animals, wind and water spread them.) Why are there so many seeds inside a pumpkin or melon? (Pumpkins and melons have a tough outer skin which rarely splits open naturally. They are harvested so that very few of the seeds ever fall to the ground naturally. Many of the seeds are thrown away as waste products. Only a few are collected for growing purposes and sown in a place where they can grow.) How can you grow a plant from a seed? (Cover it with soil and water it.)

Follow-up activities

✧ Look for the seeds of trees such as oak and horse chestnut. Break them open to compare.
✧ Watch sycamore seeds being carried to the ground on the wind. Use them as spinners or make a simple spinner with some card.
✧ Read 'Sycamore seed' by Judith Nicholls on page 70 in the Resources section.
✧ Count how many puffs it takes to blow the seeds off a dandelion clock.
✧ Make a collection of seeds from things eaten during one week. Compare and discuss before finding a way to display the collection. Search for different seeds around a safe outdoor play area.
✧ Thread the pumpkin seeds onto a length of string to make a necklace.

SEED TRAIL

• •

Objective

Geography – To make a trail of seeds.

Group size

Whole group.

What you need

Some acorns and a safe outdoor play space.

Preparation

Read the story 'Jake's tree' on page 78 in the Resources section about collecting fallen acorns. Go outdoors to collect some fallen acorns. Divide the children into two groups and make sure that there is an adult with both groups. Check the outdoor play area to ensure that it is free from hazards and that all boundaries are safe.

What to do

Show the children the acorns. Encourage them to handle and examine the acorns closely to see what they look and feel like. Explain that the seeds are going to be used as markers for the trail. Tell the children that one group are going to be the trail makers and the other group are going to be the trackers. The trail makers are going to start the activity twenty minutes ahead of the others to lay the trail before they follow.

Plot the trail around the outside play area and wait at the finish for the children who are following the trail. Plot the trail onto a simple map to use at a later date to explore the changes of scenery made during the autumn. Lay the seeds in patterns to make signals for the others to follow. Ensure that the children do not eat any of the seeds.

Discussion

Tell the children that acorns are the fruit of the oak tree. Explain that the acorn is like a nut with a hard outer shell that protects the seed inside. The seeds ripen in autumn and must get far away from the parent tree in order to grow. The acorns must break for the seed to get out. How do acorns get out of their shells? (Animals eat them or people

tread on them.) How are acorns scattered? (By animals or people.) Talk about the woodland code and remind the children that they must always be with an adult when laying trails. Why must you never eat the seeds and nuts you find outdoors? (They might be poisonous.)

Follow-up activities

✧ Remind the children of the story 'Jake's tree'. Encourage them to grow an acorn in a pot like Jake.
✧ Learn the song 'One little acorn' on page 85 of the Resources section.
✧ Use the collection of acorns to start a discussion about seed dispersal.
✧ Find a dandelion clock to blow and whisper the verse 'Dandelion whispers' on page 71 of the Resources section.
✧ Take the acorns from their cups and use them for one-to-one correspondence, asking the children to match each acorn to the correct up.
✧ Use an acorn to play 'Hunt the Acorn', hiding acorns all around the play area and asking the children to find and count ten acorns each.
✧ Take the children to see an oak tree in autumn when the acorns are falling to the ground.
✧ Make sesame and sunflower seed snacks to share after the activity.
✧ Use the photocopiable sheet 'Food for squirrel' on page 89 to match the acorns to the trees.

DEAD OR ALIVE?

Objective

Science — To discover if seeds float or sink.

Group size

Up to four children.

What you need

Different types of autumn fruits and seeds such as apple pips, sunflower seeds and acorns and a bowl of water.

Preparation

Fill the bowl with water and place on a flat surface.

What to do

Ask the children to guess which seeds will float and which seeds will sink when they are dropped into the water. Invite them to divide the seeds into two groups, one containing all the seeds they think will float, the other containing all the seeds they think will sink. Ask the children to test the seeds one at a time to find out if they float or sink by carefully placing them into the bowl of water to predict what might happen to the seeds. Segregate the seeds that have been tested.

Encourage the children to put the seeds into two piles, ones that float and ones that sink. The seeds that sink should be fertile ones; they are heavy because the fleshy part has not dried out. The seeds that float should be dead because the inside fleshy part has dried out and withered.

Remind the children never to eat seeds without an adult's consent.

Discussion

Talk to the children about seeds. Discuss how ripe seeds are ready to collect in autumn. Tell them that it is difficult to know if a seed is dead or alive. Sometimes a seed lies sleeping (dormant) for a very long time before it begins to grow. Explain that the time a seed takes to sprout varies. An acorn takes about a month, whereas other seeds can lie in the ground for over a year. Tell the children that seeds need water and light to help them grow. Ask the children to observe what happens when they put the seeds in water. Why do some seeds sink? Why do others float? (Some absorb water to make them heavy; others remain light because they have a waxy surface, which is waterproof.) What will happen if the seeds are left without light or water? (They will not grow.)

Follow-up activities

✧ Collect a variety of fresh seeds. Soak them overnight in warm water. Peel off the hard outer shells if you can and place them in pots of soil or compost. Water the seeds and place a plastic bag over the pots. Put the pots in a sunny place and wait for them to grow.
✧ Compare the growth rate of different seeds under different conditions.
✧ Grow seeds in water and watch how their roots develop.
✧ Cut the word 'autumn' from blotting paper and sow some quick-growing seeds such as cress on it.
✧ Plant some autumn bulbs and record how long it takes for them to grow.

NUTTY MIXTURES

Objective

Mathematics – To sort nuts into sets.

Group size

Three children.

What you need

Large quantities of horse chestnuts, acorns and hazelnuts, one large bowl and four small bowls.

What to do

Begin the activity by reminding the children never to eat nuts without an adult's consent. Let the children handle and examine the different nuts. Point out the differences between the horse chestnuts, acorns and hazelnuts. Explain that nuts fall down from trees in autumn.

Invite the children to put the nuts into a large bowl, mixing them together as they do so. When all the nuts are mixed together give each child a bowl and a different nut. Challenge one child to find all the horse chestnuts, another child to find all the acorns and the last remaining child to find all the hazelnuts.

Discussion

How did the nuts feel and smell? What noise did they make when you were mixing them together? (Rattled and clattered.) Compare the size of the acorn to the size of the horse chestnut. Which nut is the biggest? Which nut is the smallest?

Follow-up activities

✧ Collect horse chestnuts, acorns and hazelnuts in their shells. Open the shells to look inside.
✧ Compare the nuts with the shells. Make a list of words to describe each. Look at colour, shape, texture and size.
✧ Use the assorted nuts to carry out simple weighing activities.
✧ Learn the nursery rhyme 'I had a little nut tree' (Traditional).
✧ Collect horse chestnut seeds in their shells. Ask the children to estimate the number of conkers inside each shell. Use them for weighing activities. Thread a conker on string to play conkers.
✧ Learn the rhyme 'I'm a little conker!' on page 71 in the Resources section.

FOREST PENDANTS

Objective

Design and Technology — To design and make a symmetrically-patterned seed pendant.

Group size

Individually, in small groups of about six children.

What you need

Flat fruit seeds (such as melon and pumpkin seeds), coloured pulse beans (such as dried black beans or kidney beans), glue, a circle of card approximately 5cm in diameter, scissors and some wool.

Preparation

Collect a variety of seeds and pulses. Wash them thoroughly and spread them out on a tray to dry. Cut six circles of card (one for each child) and make a small hole in the top of each one.

What to do

Explain to the children how the seeds inside some fruit often grow in a symmetrical pattern. Cut an apple in half to demonstrate what you mean. Pointing out the seed arrangement, explain that a symmetrical pattern is one where all the parts are arranged in exact correspondence to one another.

Give each child a circle of card. Invite them to spread a thick layer of glue on it. Remind the children not to eat the seeds. Challenge them to press the seeds and pulses into the glue to make symmetrical patterns.

Leave the finished pendants to dry overnight. To make the pendant into a necklace, thread a length of wool through the hole in the circle and tie. Let the children varnish the pendants to give a more luxurious finish.

Discussion

Talk to the children about the way some people use seeds collected from the forests to make jewellery to wear or sell. Tell them that they are going to make pendants using seeds and pulses. Look at the different names, shapes and colours of the seeds. Have you ever seen a forest? What seeds might

you find in autumn? (Sycamore, horse chestnut, sunflower and pumpkin seeds.)

Follow-up activities

✧ Use autumn seeds from autumn fruits (such as apple pips) to make another pendant.
✧ Use the pendant to make a bracelet, brooch or earrings by tying it to appropriate lengths of wool.
✧ Grade a selection of seeds into sizes. Label and display them.
✧ Paint large blobs of paint in autumn colours onto a piece of white paper. Fold the paper in half and press it firmly down. Open the paper out to reveal symmetrical patterns.
✧ Look for other symmetrical patterns.
✧ Photocopy the sheet 'Rangoli patterns' on page 94 onto card and give one copy to each child. Let them glue on seeds to make a Rangoli pattern.

BERRY JUICE

Objective

Science – To learn about the changes that occur when tie-dying a piece of cloth in berry juice.

Group size

Up to four children.

What you need

A piece of white sheeting (approximately 30cm × 20cm), some autumn berries such as blackberries, a fine mesh sieve, a potato masher, some string, scissors, salt, small pebbles, a bowl, four waterproof aprons and a washing-up bowl filled with a litre of water.

Preparation

Take the children on a walk to collect a variety of autumn berries, such as hawthorn and blackberry. Warn the children about the dangers of eating berries. Put the bowl of water on a flat surface.

What to do

Give the children a piece of white cloth, some pebbles and string. Ask them to tie the pebbles separately in the cloth.

Put the berries into a bowl, pour on a little water and use the potato masher to extract the juice from the berries. Strain the mixture to remove the crushed berries. Place the cloth carefully into the dye mixture so that it is completely submerged. Leave for an hour so that the berry juice can permeate the material. Take the cloth out of the dye and leave it to dry.

Mix a cupful of salt with the water in the washing-up bowl. Plunge the cloth into the salt water and leave overnight to fix the berry-coloured dye. Take out the pebbles and dry the cloth to reveal the patterned berry stains left where the pebbles were tied up in the cloth. When the cloth is dry, mount on a piece of white card and display.

Discussion

Explain to the children that berries ripen in autumn to provide animals and birds with the food

they need to fatten up before winter. Talk about the changes that have taken place during the activity. What happened to the salt when you put it in the bowl of water? (It dissolved.) How did you extract the juice from the berries to make the dye? (Mashed them with the potato masher.) Talk about the differences between reversible changes and irreversible changes. Extracting the juices is an irreversible change because you cannot put it back, as is using salt to fix the dye so that the berry stains will not come out of the cloth. What happened to the white cloth when you put it in the berry juice? (It changed colour.) What happened when you took the pebbles out? (There were different shades and circular patterns on the cloth where the pebbles had been tied by the string.)

Follow-up activities

✧ Tie a piece of cloth at intervals along its length. Dip into berry juice. Untie the string to reveal rows of wavy patterns.
✧ Use fruit or vegetables to make different coloured dyes; onion skins produce a good autumn colour.
✧ Mash edible berries into warm water to make fruit juice.
✧ Dip kitchen paper, tissue and different kinds of absorbent paper into the berry juice to create pleasant patterns.
✧ Dip the corners of a folded paper towel quickly into saucers of food colouring. When the towel is dry open it to see symmetrical patterns.
✧ Read and learn the rhyme 'Four Scarlet Berries' from *This Little Puffin* compiled by Elizabeth Matterson (Puffin).

SHAKER SEEDS

Objective

Music – To make shakers with seeds.

Group size

Up to eight children.

What you need

Several small plastic containers with their lids, such as camera film containers and small plastic drinking bottles or shampoo bottles, sunflower seeds and some sticky tape.

Preparation

Plant and grow sunflowers ready to collect their seed heads in autumn.

What to do

Show the children the giant seed head of a sunflower and ask them to remove the seeds from it. Divide the seeds among the children.

Challenge them to sort the seeds into piles of different quantities, some with a few seeds, others with lots of seeds. Invite the children to choose a plastic container and ask them to put some of the seeds into the containers. Remind the children not to put any seeds in their mouths. Replace the cap.

Stick tape all around the top of the container to secure it firmly into place.

Make several more shakers, experimenting with the amount of seeds in each container to produce different sounds. Let the children compare the different sounds the shakers make before using them to make music.

Discussion

Explain to the children that seeds ripen in autumn, ready to grow into plants again or to be eaten by animals and birds. Tell them that the giant seed heads of a sunflower are a treasure-trove for birds because they contain hundreds of seeds for them to eat. Discuss the way shakers make music. Which shakers make the lowest/loudest sounds? (The ones containing lots of seeds.) Which shakers make the highest/quietest sounds? (The ones with fewer seeds.)

Follow-up activities

✧ Collect and sort a variety of seeds such as apple pips, acorns and melon seeds and use them to make different sounding shakers.

✧ Grade the shakers according to high or low notes and according to loud or quiet sounds. Record by making a sound chart.

✧ Decorate the shakers according to a topical theme such as autumn shades, fruits or the sounds they make.

✧ Use the shakers to accompany a song and dance.

✧ Make up a song about seeds or the autumn season to sing along to the shaker music.

SCATTER SEEDS

● ●

Objective

PE / dance – To dance like scattering seeds.

Group size

Whole group.

What you need

Some grass seeds, a safe outdoor space (preferably with a patch of earth on which to scatter the seeds), a clear indoor space (large enough for the children to dance around freely).

Preparation

Check that the areas being used for this activity are safe and free from hazards. Give the children a handful of seeds to scatter outdoors, to give them firsthand knowledge of what happens to seeds when they are scattered.

What to do

Talk to the children about the way the farmers scatter seeds during autumn. Explain that the actions used by farmers during autumn to sow their seeds can be linked in rhythmic movement phrases to make a dance.

Demonstrate the movements made by farmers when they are scattering and gathering seeds. Show the children the way farmers stoop, lift and walk in a repetitive pattern as they gather in the seeds. Give the children time to practise this phrasing several times until they are familiar with it. Encourage them to make up their own movement phrases based upon the way seeds are scattered. Invite the children to practise individually before making up a group dance.

Use harvest music such as 'Oats and Beans and Barley Grow' from *This Little Puffin* compiled by Elizabeth Matterson (Puffin) or 'We Plough the Fields and Scatter' (Traditional hymn) to accompany the dance. Groups of children could dance different phrases at the same time to give added dimensions to the dance.

Discussion

What happens to the seeds when you scatter them? (They fall to the ground.) What happens to the seeds after they fall to the ground? (Some grow.) Why do only a few of the seeds grow? (Only some land on good growing ground.) What happens to the seeds that do not grow? (Birds and animals eat them.) What happens to the seeds that grow? (They grow into plants again.)

Follow-up activities

✧ Tell the parable of the farmer and the seeds from the Bible.
✧ Use simple reference books to discover how farmers harvest crops. Invite the children to imitate the movements made by the machinery they see in the pictures.
✧ Plant sunflower seeds and watch them grow.
✧ Cover a piece of paper with glue and scatter some mixed seeds on it to make a textured pattern.
✧ Collect and grow a variety of seeds; keep a record of how long they take to grow.

CHAPTER 5
AUTUMN GAMES

Autumn offers the chance to play traditional games, dress up and wear masks. Activities in this chapter include apple bobbing, filling boxes with nature's provisions and playing a game with autumn words. Children can also go on a wild leaf chase, close their eyes to discover the beauty of autumn and play a lift-the-flap memory game.

BOB AN APPLE

Objective

Science – To find out if apples float or sink.

Group size

Up to eight children.

What you need

A washing-up bowl, a towel, water, an apple for each child taking part and a flat, low surface.

Preparation

Read the poem 'Apple bobbing' on page 72 as stimulus for this activity before you start the game.

What to do

Fill a clean washing-up bowl with water. Give the children an apple each and invite them to take turns to put their apple in the bowl of water. When all the apples are floating in the water, tell the children to hold their hands behind their backs. Challenge them to take turns to retrieve the apple from the bowl with their mouth.

This game is much trickier than it looks but it is great fun to play. Look at the characteristics of water. Ask the children to let it run through their fingers to discover that water needs to be contained. Examine the wetness of water by touching and dripping it.

Discussion

Explain that the apple is one of the most important fruits of autumn. They are often used in autumn games such as bobbing for an apple. Do apples float or sink? (Float.) Talk to the children about the way apples float in the water. Why does an apple float? (It is lighter than water and it has a glossy skin that prevents the water from being absorbed.) Why is it difficult to grab the apple in your mouth? (The water makes it slippery.) Is water wet or dry? What else is wet? Where does water come from? What happens when apples are left in water for a long time? (As apples rot, the skin breaks allowing it to soak up water.) What happens if the apple soaks up water? (It becomes heavy and sinks.)

Follow-up activities

✧ Collect autumn fruits to test if they float or sink.
✧ Start a collection of pictures with apples in them.
✧ Read the story 'Little Bear's Toffee Apples' in *A Year Full of Stories 366 Stories and Poems* Georgia Adams and Selina Young (Orion).
✧ Make apple prints.
✧ Cut large apple shapes from card and staple them together to make a book about apples.

FILL THE FOREST

Objective

Mathematics – To play a sorting game about autumn themes.

Group size

Four children.

What you need

Large sheets of thin card, some scissors, four large empty shoe boxes, felt-tipped crayons and a room with a clear, central space.

Preparation

Cut slits in the boxes big enough to post the cards through. Label the boxes according to the autumn themes you are studying such as 'Tree', 'Fruit', 'Weather' and 'Animal'. Draw a diagram on the box to represent each word. Cut some thin card into 20 rectangles measuring approximately 8cm × 3cm. Draw pictures of the objects associated with each box on the cards. Make up four sets of cards.

What to do

Give the children a box with a different picture on it. Show them the four sets of cards. Explain that each set of cards has different pictures on them to match the ones on the boxes. For example, all the cards with trees or parts of trees belong in the box with a tree on it and so on.

Scatter all the cards face down around the room. Tell the children to place their boxes in a different corner of the room. Challenge them to find the five cards that belong in their box. When they have found all five cards, ask them to post them one at a time into the correct box. When they have finished posting all the cards call the children back together. Empty the boxes one at a time to check that the children have collected and posted the correct cards.

Repeat the game several times so that the children have the opportunity to post cards into all four boxes. Each time remind the children to post the cards into the correct boxes.

Discussion

Why does the card with a branch on it go into the box with a picture of a tree? (It is part of a tree.) Which cards go into the box with an animal on it? (All the cards with animals on them.) How many cards are you going to post into your box? (Five.)

Follow-up activities

✧ Use the cards for table-top sorting activities.
✧ Use the boxes to play a similar game but choose a different theme such as 'Fill the Zoo' or 'Fill the Larder'.
✧ Base the game on making cakes. Mark boxes with the names of different cakes such as 'chocolate muffins', 'fruit cake', 'jam sponge' and 'flapjacks'. Write the matching ingredients onto separate cards. Invite the children to take it in turns to find the ingredients to make their cake.
✧ Play a word association game about autumn.

DROP STICKS, PICK UP STICKS

• •

Objective

PE – To play a jumping game.

Group size

Whole group.

What you need

A safe outdoor play area, some fallen twigs and half a metre of red ribbon.

Preparation

Make a 'medal' with a small twig, together with a piece of red ribbon.

What to do

Take the children outdoors after a windy night to collect fallen twigs. Examine them and encourage the children to notice all the characteristics of twigs. Explain that you are going to play a game with them that is based on the way horse-trainers use trotting-poles.

Lay six twigs on the ground about 30cm apart. Take it in turns to trot over the twigs without touching them. Challenge the children to play trotting-twigs in the form of a competition.

The last child to go, jumps as far as possible over the last twig and calls out a number from one to six while jumping. If that child calls 'three', for example, then twig number three is moved to the spot where the child lands. There is now a big space between twigs two and four and between twigs five and six.

Continue the game in the same way, taking it in turns to be the last jumper. If you knock a stick or if you cannot jump over the space between them, you are out. The child left in at the end of the game is the trotting twig champion. Award the winning child the medal you have made.

Discussion

Explain that sometimes, in autumn, when there has been a storm, twigs get blown down from the trees. Tell the children that you can tell the age of

a twig by counting the circular markings on a cross-section through the middle of it, and by the girdle marks along the outside left by yearly growth. Tell the children that twigs have annual rings like tree trunks. How old is your twig? (Count the number of rings.) How many girdle scars can you see on the outside of the twig? Do they all agree? Have you ever been out for a walk on an autumn day after a storm? What was it like? What did you see? Have you ever seen the rings inside a fallen tree trunk?

Follow-up activities

✧ Wind several shades of autumn-coloured wool around twigs to make a woven sculpture.
✧ Make imprints of small twigs by pressing them firmly into clay or playdough.
✧ Make casts of the twig imprints by taping a strip of cardboard all around the sides of the tile bearing the imprint. Pour in plaster of Paris and leave overnight to dry. Peel away the cardboard to reveal the cast. Paint the cast in natural colours.

WORDS OF AUTUMN

Objective

English — To make a list of autumn words.

Group size

Whole group.

What you need

Paper, scissors, and a broad-tipped marker pen.

Preparation

Make 20 silhouettes of an object that reminds the children of autumn, such as an acorn. Cut them out and keep them ready to play the game.

What to do

Invite the children to talk about their own experiences and memories of autumn. Ask them to think of different words to describe their experiences. Talk about the season of autumn and all the things it brings to mind. Give the children a few examples such as fallen leaves, frost and acorns to help them understand the concept.

Write the words suggested clearly on the silhouette shapes. Write each word on a separate acorn-shaped card and invite the children to tell you about their experiences of autumn until you have a long list of words. Put the cards into a pile face down and pick up the top card. Describe the word written on the card to the children without actually saying it and encourage them to guess what the word is. Older children will be able to write and read the words for themselves, describing to the rest of the group.

Discussion

Talk to the children about their experiences of autumn. What do you think about when you hear the word autumn? What words can you use to describe autumn? What do you like most about autumn? What do you not like about autumn? What animals do you see outdoors in autumn? (Squirrels.) What happens to trees in autumn? What is the weather like in autumn?

Follow-up activities

✧ Make up two sets of the cards to play a matching game.
✧ Draw a picture on the back of each card to illustrate the word on it.
✧ Cut out a large silhouette of a tree and write or draw all the words and objects associated with trees on it. Do the same with large silhouettes of such objects as apples, acorns and hedgehogs. Use them to make an autumn display.
✧ Hide all the cards face down around the play area. Give the children ten seconds to retrieve them. The child with the most cards wins the game.
✧ Make ten small cards in an autumn shape as before. Number the cards 1 to 10. Hide corresponding objects in a sand tray. Invite the children to pick a card with a number on it. Challenge them to find the same number of objects as the number on their card.

WILD LEAF CHASE

Objective

Geography — To make a trail with fallen leaves.

Group size

Whole group.

What you need

Four leaves (two of each kind of two obviously different leaves such as an oak, a horse chestnut or a beech leaf), four pieces of card approximately 15cm × 20cm, glue, a roll of clear sticky plastic and some small pebbles or stones.

Preparation

Identify a safe area in the school grounds or nearby where there are plenty of trees. Make sure you choose leaves from the trees growing in the environment where the activity takes place to ensure that there are plenty of the same leaves lying around the area for the children to collect. Stick the leaves onto separate pieces of card. Cover the cards with a clear, sticky-backed plastic when they are dry.

What to do

Divide the children into two groups. Give each group a different set of leaf cards. Send them off together to collect as many leaves as they can find to match the one on their card. After ten minutes, call the children back together.

Invite one group to use the leaves they have found to lay a trail for the other group to follow. Encourage the children to place a small stone or pebble on top of each leaf to hold it in place. At the end of each trail, tell the children to hide one of their cards for the others to find. Challenge the other group of children to find the hidden card by following the leaf trail. Tell the children to use one of the cards to compare with the leaves marking the trail to ensure that they are going the right way. When the first group finds the card, repeat the process, but swap roles so that all the children experience both setting and following a trail.

Discussion

How can you tell you are going the right way? (The leaf stuck on the card matches the ones on the trail.) What happens to the leaves when there is a strong wind blowing? (They blow away.) How can you make sure the leaves marking the trail stay in place? (Put something heavy on them such as a stone or pebble.)

Follow-up activities

✧ Hide some treasure for the children to find at the end of each trail.
✧ Let the trail lead the children to a picnic to share at the end.
✧ Use other autumn objects such as horse chestnuts or acorns as markers for the trail.
✧ Tell the story of *Hansel and Gretel* (Traditional).

I CLOSE MY EYES

Objective

Music – To play a musical game to help recognize and perform variations in tempo.

Group size

Whole group.

What you need

A place to play quietly.

What to do

Divide the group into 'owls' and 'squirrels'. Let the children imagine that they are high up in the branches of trees during autumn.

Make the following sounds to accompany the words you are saying to the children:

· 'I'm moving along a branch' – slap hands on knees quickly.

· 'I'm sleeping' – snoring sound with head resting on hands.

· 'I'm washing myself' – licking sound.

· 'I'm preparing for take off' – arms flapping against sides.

· 'I need to scratch' – scratching sound.

Make the sounds one at a time quickly or slowly. Tell the children to close their eyes, to listen carefully and to join in with the slow sounds if they are the sleepy 'owls' and the fast sounds if they are 'squirrels'. Let the 'owls' take a turn at being the 'squirrels' and vice versa. Aim for a big contrast in the speed when you say the phrases so that the children can grasp the concept of the game.

Discussion

Tell the children that woodland animals move at different speeds in autumn. Some of them move slowly so they put on weight to build up fat stores for the long winter months ahead or because they are sleepy in preparation for hibernation. The owl moves very slowly, if at all, during the day because it is resting ready to go out searching for food at night. The squirrel is a naturally speedy animal.

How can you tell when the owl is moving along a branch? (The sounds are slow.) How can you tell when the squirrel is moving along the branch? (The sounds are fast.) When do you know that the owl has gone to sleep? (The snoring noises are slow.) When do you know that the squirrel is thirsty? (The lapping sounds are fast.) When do you know that the owl is hungry? (The chewing sounds are slow.) How can you tell which animal is scratching? (If the scratching sounds are slow the owl is scratching, if the sounds are fast the squirrel is scratching.)

Follow-up activities

✧ Introduce another woodland animal to the game, such as a badger, which would move at an intermediate speed.

✧ Tie a piece of rope around the trunk of a tree. Give the children an eye mask. Tell them to use the rope as a guide while you lead them slowly around the tree trunk. Encourage them to feel the texture of the bark. Let them use the rope guide to walk around the tree without help. Discuss how they feel. Walk around the same tree quickly and then run around it.

✧ Play 'Kim's game' but pretend to take the objects very quickly as if you are a squirrel, or slowly as if you are a sleepy owl.

✧ Take the children outdoors to listen to the sounds of autumn such as animals running along branches or leaves falling from trees.

RATTLE CLATTER WIND CHIMES

Objective

Design and Technology — To find ways of tying objects to string in order to make wind chimes.

Group size

Four to six children.

What you need

A collection of autumnal items such as acorns and conkers with holes cut or drilled in them, metal spoons, a piece of rope tied safely between two objects to make a line, six pieces of string approximately 30cm long and a variety of string, thread and wool to practise tying knots.

Preparation

Go outdoors with the children for this activity. Tie the rope between two strong objects to make a washing line. Show the children some basic knots. Give the children some lengths of string and encourage them to experiment with tying knots. Read the poem 'Who am I?' about the wind on page 67 in the Resources section.

What to do

Give each child a piece of string and an acorn or conker and invite them to tie the string onto the acorn/conker so that it is secure and will not fall off. Tie the acorns and conkers along the rope at

well-spaced intervals, just high enough for the children to reach them. Encourage the children to make musical sounds by gently tapping the acorns and conkers together with the spoons.

Leave the chimes outdoors during a windy autumn day and encourage the children to listen to the sounds made by the items rattling and clanking together. Encourage the children to move when they hear the sounds of the chimes and to stand still when the chimes are silent.

Discussion

Ask the children to listen carefully. Can you hear the wind? How can you tell when the wind is blowing? (The leaves and branches will be moving on the trees or swirling to the ground.) What happens to the acorns and conkers when the wind blows them together? (They make clattering sounds.) How can you make sounds with the wind chimes? (Bang them gently with the spoon.)

Follow-up activities

✧ Use different materials such as cotton, wool or string to tie objects to compare their different properties.
✧ Hang a variety of different-sized objects such as metal or wooden spoons, foil, hollow wooden or metal tubes or plastic bottles. Leave outdoors on a windy autumn day and listen to them rattling and clattering in the autumn wind.
✧ Dangle leaves tied on string from the line. Listen to them quietly rustling in the wind.
✧ Make paper windmills and kites to blow around in the wind.

AUTUMN'S PASSED

Objective

History – To make and play a 'lift-the-flap' memory game.

Group size

Whole group.

What you need

A sheet of sugar paper, thin white card, scissors, glue, coloured felt-tipped pens.

Preparation

Draw the outline of an oak tree onto a piece of sugar paper and cut out 12 large acorn shapes from thin card.

What to do

Give each child an acorn shape and ask them to draw a picture to represent autumn. Very young children could make a pattern with autumn colours; others could make a representational drawing of an autumn scene or object. Ask the children to glue their acorns onto the outline of the tree to make 'lift-the-flap' windows with them.

Ask the children to remember all the things they enjoy most about the autumn. Encourage the children in turn to talk to the group about their own special memory of autumn. Jot down a simple phrase under the children's acorn pictures to record their memory. Older children could write their own descriptions. Lift the acorn flaps in random order. Read the phrase written underneath the flap. Ask the children to remember who said it. Remind the child whose description you are reading to remain quiet until the others have made a guess.

Discussion

Ask the children to think about the things they have experienced or noticed about autumn. What do you like best about autumn? What do you like doing most during autumn? What smells remind you most of autumn? (Burning leaves, roasting chestnuts or toffee apples.) What sounds remind you of autumn? (Rustling leaves or the wind blowing.) What is the most exciting thing that has happened to you during autumn? (Collecting conkers, a party, walking in the woods.)

Follow-up activities

✧ Decorate a twig with autumn objects to make an 'autumn tree' as a celebration of the season.
✧ Take photographs during autumn to make a memory book to look at together.
✧ Glue pictures of objects associated with autumn underneath the acorns. Ask the children to guess what is hiding underneath each acorn.

CHAPTER 6
AUTUMN CELEBRATIONS

Enjoy some autumnal festivals and celebrations by making Mexican sugar shapes, festive lanterns and Lammas loaves. Uncover the legend of wandering Jack, celebrate Japanese New Taste Festival and make a traditional mask.

MEXICAN SUGAR SHAPES

Objective

Design and Technology – To design and decorate biscuits.

Group size

Four children.

What you need

Six plain biscuits, icing sugar, water, mixing bowl, tablespoon, small tubes of different-coloured piping to decorate.

Preparation

Mix the icing sugar into a thick paste with two tablespoons of water. Decorate one of the biscuits to use as a sample to show the children what to do. Begin with a general discussion about making gifts for each other. Tell the children that people from other countries like to give special presents too and that sugar skulls made from icing sugar are given as gifts of thanks at harvest time in Mexico. Demonstrate how to make the biscuit into a special gift as you are talking to the children.

What to do

Give the children a biscuit each and invite them to cover it with some of the icing sugar. Leave the iced biscuit for ten minutes to dry. When the icing is dry, challenge the children to use tubes of coloured sugar gel to decorate their iced biscuits, making a face on the icing. (The face represents the Mexican sugar skull.) Put to one side to dry. Later give the special biscuits as presents.

Discussion

Talk to the children about making and giving special presents. What is your favourite present? Who would you most like to give your special biscuit to? Why do you want to give it to them? When do you usually give or receive presents? (Birthdays, Christmas, to say thank you or to celebrate special occasions.)

Follow-up activities

✧ Decorate biscuits with other topical designs such as autumn berries, nuts and flowers or hearts and kisses.
✧ Use typical autumn fruit as a topping for the thank you biscuits.
✧ Make other thank you gifts.
✧ Wrap an object associated with autumn in a box to play a guessing game.
✧ Share the decorated biscuits.
✧ Learn and sing the song 'Make a face' in *Game-songs with Prof Dogg's Troupe* Harriet Powell (A & C Black).

HARVEST CARDS

Objective

RE – To make harvest thank you cards.

Group size

Up to eight children.

What you need

A picture or example of a traditional corn or rice dolly, some card, a collection of dried grasses (corn, barley, wheat, oats, rice), glue, scissors and coloured marker pens.

Preparation

Show the children the pictures or samples of the corn and rice dollies and explain that they were made as good luck charms or thanksgiving symbols to encourage plentiful harvests. Discuss how they were made and what materials were used.

What to do

Collect samples of different dried grasses and corn such as wheat, oats and barley. Discuss their characteristics and make observational pencil drawings to record what the grasses look like. Use the grasses to make traditional corn dollies or rice babies using the samples as guidelines.

Fold the card in half. Arrange sheaves or grasses on the front surface of the card or use the corn dollies as the main design. Glue into place and leave to dry. Use as a card to express thanks for nature's gift of food at harvest time. Older children can write their messages of thanks to the recipients inside the cards.

Discussion

Talk about the different types of grasses. Which ones are long? Which ones are short? Which ones are straight? Which ones are curved? Which ones are thick? Which ones are thin? Tell the children about the harvesting of corn and how it is used to make food. Explain that corn dollies and rice babies were made with the last stalks of corn. Tell the children that they were hung up to bring good luck to the next harvest.

Follow-up activities

✧ Ask the children to draw the shape of a body on a piece of card. Glue rice inside the outline to make a rice dolly.
✧ Look at the ingredients on boxes of cereals to discover which ones contain wheat, oats or rice.
✧ Make a chart to show which breakfast cereals are the most popular.
✧ Sing 'Oats and Beans and Barley Grow' from *This Little Puffin* compiled by Elizabeth Matterson (Puffin). Learn actions to go with the song or play along to it with percussion instruments.
✧ Make cards in the shape of harvest food such as apples, pears or bread.
✧ Use the grasses to make small harvest gifts such as bookmarks, table mats and mounted pictures.
✧ Take the children to a traditional harvest festival.

PUNKIE LANTERNS

Objective

History — To make traditional punkie lanterns from vegetables.

Group size

Four children.

What you need

Turnips (one for each child taking part), ballpoint pens, pieces of string for a handle, glue, carrot, a paring knife and four spoons.

Preparation

Make up a sample of a turnip lantern before the activity to show the children.

What to do

First slice off the top of the turnip but do not throw it away. Give the children a spoon and invite them to scoop out the flesh inside the turnip taking care not to break the skin. Younger children may need some help to do this.

Using the ballpoint pens, ask the children to draw eyes, a nose and a mouth to make a face on the turnips. Cut out the shapes they have drawn to make a face on the lantern. Pierce two holes either side of the head. Thread the string through to make a carrying handle. Then replace the top to make a lid.

Discussion

Tell the children that long ago women were worried that the men bringing in the crops had not returned home from work. They decided to go looking for them but as the men had taken all the lanterns with them, the women had to make their own rough lanterns out of turnips to light their way. It has become tradition to make punkie lanterns. Where do turnips grow? (Underground.) Have you ever seen a turnip before? Have you eaten turnip? Do you know the names of any other vegetables that grow underground? (Potato, carrot, swede and parsnip.)

Follow-up activities

✧ Learn the traditional punkie chant 'It's punkie night tonight, it's punkie night tonight. Give us a candle, give us a light. It's punkie night tonight'.
✧ Make a collection of root vegetables.
✧ Make lanterns with other vegetables such as pumpkins and swedes.
✧ Use the vegetable flesh to make soup.
✧ Read the English folk tale 'The Boggart' from the book *Festivals Together* (Hawthorne Press).
✧ Sing 'This Little Light of Mine' (Traditional).

LAMMAS LOAVES

* *

Objective

RE – To make traditional Lammas loaves from sliced bread.

Group size

Four children.

What you need

Ten slices of wholemeal bread, a paring knife, spread such as butter, Marmite or honey.

Preparation

Use two slices of bread to make a Lammas loaf or have a harvest loaf or a picture of traditional harvest loaves as a sample to show the children. Begin with a general discussion about harvest bread, encouraging the children to draw on their own experiences about sharing food and giving at harvest time.

What to do

Give each child a plate, paring knife and some spread. Invite them to join the slices of bread together to make a sandwich. Encourage the children to cut round shapes from their sandwiches to represent traditional Lammas loaves.

Discussion

Explain to the children that the first sheaves of wheat were made into special loaves called Lammas loaves on 1 August to say thank you for a good harvest. The first day of harvest is called Loafmas day. The first loaf was made in a special design and used as decoration or to share during the celebrations of the first harvest of the year.

Follow-up activities

✧ Use a dough mix to make bread in the shape of a Lammas loaf.
✧ Take the children to a baker's shop to see a traditional harvest loaf being made.
✧ Buy a variety of unusual bread to share.
✧ Sing 'Five Currant Buns' but change the words to 'Five Lammas Loaves'.
✧ Make a Lammas loaf from salt dough, varnish it to preserve and use as a prop for imaginative play.

LACY LANTERNS

Objective

Art – To make a paper lantern.

Group size

Up to four children.

What you need

Thin white paper, stiff paper, a dinner plate, yellow, red and orange marbling paints, a shallow tray, scissors, string, glue.

Preparation

Pour the marbling paints into the tray and swirl them around to mix them together. Before you begin this activity, read the poem 'Lanterns' on page 73 in the Resources section.

What to do

Give each child a sheet of the thin white paper. Invite them to dip it into the tray of marbling paints to create swirling patterns in the autumnal shades. Leave on a flat surface for a couple of hours to dry.

Place the plate on the painted paper and make two circular templates. Cut out the circles. Fold each circle three times and make deep cuts from the sides and open flat. Glue small circles of stiff paper to the centre of each. When dry, make a hole in the centre of one of them and thread with string. Knot both ends to make a loop. Turn the other circle over and press spots of glue on every other fold. Press the circle with the loop down onto the sticky circle. When dry, gently tease apart to make a lacy lantern.

Discussion

Can you remember how the lanterns were described in the poem? Can you remember some of the words used? (Glowing, delicate, vivid colours.) What are lanterns used for? Where could we hang our lanterns?

Follow-up activities

✧ Make lots of small lacy lanterns and attach them to a coat-hanger using different lengths of string to make a mobile.
✧ Make lacy table mats with circles of card cut in the same way but taking small chunks out of the folded circles instead of making slits.
✧ Make flakes of autumn sunlight in the same way but colour the card in bright autumn colours.
✧ Mount white lacy circles onto bright green, orange and yellow card to display.
✧ Use the photocopiable sheet 'Paper lantern' on page 95 to make a Chinese paper lantern.

WANDERING JACK

Objective

PE/Dance – To create a dance to help Jack change his luck to find a resting place.

Group size

Whole group.

What you need

An open space.

What to do

Explain to the children that the faint mist sometimes seen just above the ground on still autumn nights, just after sunset, looks like a flickering light.

Tell them that there is an old folk tale about a young boy called Jack who got lost on the moors. Every time he bumped into a spider's web he turned round to run the other way. The swirling mist is supposed to be poor, luckless Jack forever wandering around looking for his way home. Sometimes the dancing shapes made by the mist are called Jack o' Lantern.

Invite the children to move like Jack, the wandering boy who is forever lost in a mist. Encourage them to duck and dive out of the way of spider's webs before spinning around to go off in another direction. Suggest that the children change Jack's luck by finding a place for him to rest. Extend the activity by giving the children silver and white streamers to create the effect of the Jack o' Lantern flickering in the mist.

Discussion

Tell the children that spiders' webs are common in autumn because the autumn countryside swarms with spiders. Explain that spiders spin webs that look like silken blankets covering everything. Have you ever seen a spider's web? What did it look like? (Lace, silky blankets.) Why do you think Jack get lost in the mist?

Follow-up activities

✧ Make lace patterns like webs by cutting deep slits into a circular piece of folded paper. Open it and press flat.
✧ Make a spider's web by winding white thread around pegs in a pegboard or around pieces of fallen twig.
✧ Go outdoors on an autumn day to count the number of spider's webs you can find.
✧ Visit a museum to look at an old spinning wheel.
✧ Learn the rhyme 'Incy Wincy Spider Climbed Up the Water Spout' from *This Little Puffin* compiled by Elizabeth Matterson (Puffin).

JAPANESE NEW TASTE FESTIVAL

Objective

English — To play a sensory game and learn about the autumn celebrations of other cultures.

Group size

Four to six children.

What you need

Boiled rice, strong flavoured foods (jam, honey, chocolate powder, Marmite, curry powder, sultanas, fruit, vegetables, different herbs and spices), six teaspoons, tissues to wipe sticky fingers.

Preparation

Make up some different flavoured rice, adding sweet and savoury foods to alter its taste, and spoon into small pots. Label each pot with the flavours that were added and turn the pots around so that the children cannot see the labels. Read the poem 'New taste festival' on page 73 of the Resources section.

What to do

Take care to ensure that none of the children are allergic to any of the foodstuffs they taste. Ask the children to close their eyes while you give them a taste of the rice mixtures. Use a spare spoon for each child taking part. Ask the children to guess what they are tasting.

Discussion

Tell the children that in Japan they have an important autumn festival called the New Taste Festival. This is a time of thanksgiving to celebrate the end of harvest on 23 November. In olden times, rice from the new harvest was not supposed to be eaten until after the festival. The Japanese make a rice doll in honour of the first fruits of the harvest. What does rice taste like? Do you like the taste of it? Do you prefer the rice with sweet flavours or the savoury rice? Have you tried rice dishes before? What kind of rice do you like to eat?

Follow-up activities

✧ Make sweet and savoury rice dishes to share.
✧ Make a traditional Japanese rice doll by gluing rice onto a cardboard silhouette.
✧ Put a cup full of rice into an old sock. Tie a knot tightly to make a beanbag.
✧ Colour rice with food colouring and use it to glue onto card to make an autumn mosaic picture.
✧ Go outdoors and scatter a handful of rice over your shoulder to make an autumn wish, at the same time as providing food for the birds.

GUISER'S MASK

Objective

History – To make a traditional mask.

Group size

Two to four children.

What you need

A piece of card 30cm square, strips of black or brown paper or stands of wool for hair, crayons or felt-tipped pens, 1m of elastic, scissors and glue.

Preparation .

Show the children a collection of ready-made masks, or pictures of masks, to give them some basic ideas.

What to do

Invite the children to draw a large face on a piece of card and cut it out. Measure it against their face to see if it fits. Make marks to show where eyes, nose and mouth should be. Ask the children to draw in these features before you cut them out. When you have cut them, tell the children to outline around the holes with the felt-tipped pens to make them stand out. Draw in all the other features of a face. Glue on strips of paper or the wool for hair, to make eyebrows, a moustache and/or a beard. Make a hole either side of the face and thread the elastic through the holes. Tie at the back to fit the head and make the mask secure.

Discussion

Explain that the word 'guiser' is a traditional name given to a person hiding behind a mask to disguise their real personality. (Guiser or Guizer is short for 'disguiser'.) Why do you think people wear masks? (As a disguise to prevent other people from knowing whom they really are.) When would you wear a mask? (For a party, for dressing up, for festivals or for plays.) Do you know of any famous people who wore masks? (Guy Fawkes.)

Follow-up activities

✧ Make masks with different expressions.
✧ Make masks to represent different cultures and customs.
✧ Wear a mask to tell a story in keeping with the characters portrayed, for example, a wolf mask to accompany the story of Little Red Riding Hood.
✧ Make a guiser doll by stuffing an old sock and tying it at the end. Make several different masks to change its disguise. Use the doll as a prop when telling a story.

CHAPTER 7
DISPLAYS

Displays reflect what is happening in your group, informing parents and visitors and providing an opportunity to extend children's learning while reinforcing their feelings of ownership. Make sure that you include examples of all children's work and avoid setting trends. This chapter gives some basic guidelines for displaying children's work, alongside four ideas for specific autumn displays.

DISPLAYING CHILDREN'S WORK

Putting children's work on display shows that it is appreciated and valued for its own worth. It provides parents and visitors with information about what is happening in the group and can provide a springboard for conversation as children discuss their work and explain it to their friends and family. Displaying work encourages children to take pride in what they are doing as well as developing further interest in the current topic.

Use displays as a focal point to brighten up your room adding colour and interest to the décor. The children will be particularly enthusiastic if they are given the opportunity to help assemble the display. Ongoing interest will be assured if the display is an interactive one, requiring the children's involvement once it has been put up.

Mount the work for display in a professional way, occasionally double-mounting special pieces to show them off to their best advantage. The borders around the mounted work should be cut thinly so as not to detract from the work itself.

Encourage the children to help create backdrops for displays, using such techniques as sponge-painting, bubble-painting and rubbings or by adding borders made from finger-painting, hand prints, leaf prints, vegetable or fruit prints.

Achieve added interest by using drapes, corrugated card, shiny paper, wallpaper, newsprint and different-textured materials and by displaying the work on different levels. An interactive display where children can follow instructions, lift flaps or handle objects will ensure continued interest.

Labels should be large and clear, written in a thick felt-tipped pen or printed in large letters. Mount labels on a contrasting coloured card or draw a small margin around the edge using a dark marker pen and a ruler.

The shape of the lettering and headings should be in keeping with the topic of the display itself. It is a good idea to make sure that the whole display is linked in some way to the theme it portrays.

It is important that you are not judgmental in choosing work to display and that you do not encourage children to merely aim to produce work for display purposes only. At one time or another, choose all the children's work to go on display rather than only showing work which you consider to be the best.

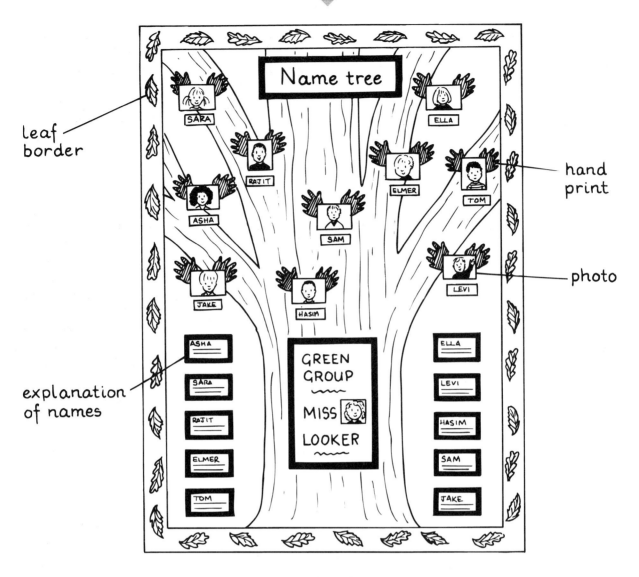

NAME TREE

What you need

Pale coloured backing paper, two pieces of orange sugar paper, ready-made paints in autumn colours, a paintbrush, large brown wax crayons, several sheets of white A4 paper (one for each child) corrugated cardboard, scissors, sticky tape, drawing pins, staple gun, strips of white card approximately 12cm wide, a small photograph of each child.

What to do

Fit the backing paper to your display board and pin leaves around the edge to make a border.

Ask the children to bring in a small photograph of themselves or take some yourself. Give each child a piece of white A4 paper. Invite the children to use the paint to make a print of each hand. Set the hand prints to one side until they are dry.

Cut a trunk and branches from the corrugated card, and encourage the children to use a brown wax crayon sideways to produce a bark effect. Position the tree in the centre of the display board.

Invite the children to cut out their hand prints to make leaves for the tree. Stick these to the display, with the children's photographs between their hand print leaves. Write the child's name on a label underneath the photograph.

Discussion

Read out the names of the children in the group. This display links with the activity, 'Branching out' on page 31. Ask the children about their different names. Why were you given your special name? Is there a story about your name? Do you know the meaning of your name? Is there anyone else with the same name as you?

UNDERGROUND, OVERGROUND

What you need

Light blue backing paper, dark brown backing paper, white paper, black marker pen, pencil, scissors, coloured felt-tipped pens, glue, staple gun, drawing pins, various sizes of cardboard tubes (cut in half lengthways), wool, string, tissue paper, corrugated card, brown paint, household decorating paintbrush, bits of string or wool and other collage materials.

What to do

Cut the top edge of the brown backing paper unevenly to represent the ground. Staple this and the light blue backing paper, which represents the sky, to the display area. Using a large household decorating brush, invite the children to paint some tree trunks and branches of varying sizes at intervals along the display area, using the join in the backing papers as the ground line. Paint roots beneath each tree. Make leaf prints in autumn colours and attach them to the branches.

Paint some large halved cardboard tubes brown on both sides and leave to dry. Attach these to the display in between the painted trunks to make three-dimensional trees. Use tubes inside out to represent tunnels made underground by creatures such as worms, rabbits and badgers. Encourage the children to make animals that should have created the tunnels and display these.

Discussion

This display links with the activities 'Home to hibernate' on page 21, 'Who's been here?' on page 23 and 'Crafty cones' on page 24. Talk to the children about animals that make burrows or live underground. Which animals live underground? (Rabbits, badgers, worms and moles.) What do you think it would be like to live underground? What things would you see underground that you couldn't see above ground? (Train tunnels, pipes from buildings, cables, animal homes.) How would you know where you were going if you lived underground? (By touch and smell.) What part of a tree grows underground? (Roots.) What part of a tree grows above the ground? (Trunk, branches and leaves.)

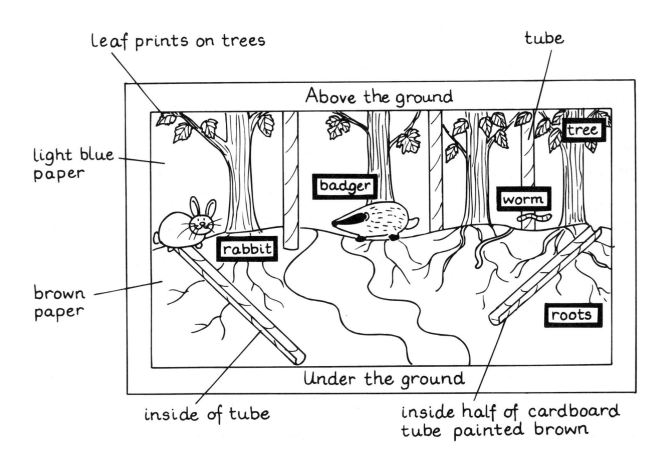

- corrugated tree shape
- rockets made with coloured foil, Cellophane streamers
- silhouettes of buildings (black sugar paper)
- road
- cereal boxes painted black
- black cereal box houses
- leaves scattered along road

The sky at night

THE SKY AT NIGHT

What you need

Black and grey sugar paper, corrugated cardboard, fluorescent paints, black paints, paintbrushes, yellow gummed paper, stapler, silver card, coloured foil, shiny card, cereal packets, scissors, fallen leaves and conkers, drawing pins, glue and sticky tape.

Preparation

Mix up the paints and cover the table with black sugar paper. Cut out a long grey 'road' and glue it to the table on top of the black sugar paper. Write and mount the sign 'The sky at night'.

What to do

Ask the children to splatter the fluorescent paint onto the black sugar paper to represent fireworks on Bonfire Night, and attach to the display board. Cut the corrugated cardboard into two tree shapes and staple to either side of the board. Encourage the children to cut out squares and rectangles from the black and grey sugar paper to represent buildings on the skyline. Staple the grey 'road' along the bottom of the board.

Paint the cereal boxes black. When they are dry, stick on squares and rectangles cut from yellow gummed paper to represent lighted windows. Staple to the display board to make a row of houses. Let the children cut silhouettes of people from black sugar paper to stick just behind the row of houses as if they are watching the fireworks.

Cut out a circle and some triangles from the silver card to make the moon and stars. Cover the cardboard tubes with coloured foil to make rockets, and attach streamers of foil or coloured Cellophane to the inside of the tubes.

Place the table in front of the display. Add more houses made from cereal boxes along the sugar paper road. Scatter fallen leaves among the houses.

Discussion

What are the people in the streets looking at? (The firework display.) How can you tell it is night? (It is dark and the lights are on in the houses.) What is happening? (It is Bonfire Night and fireworks are lighting up the sky.) Where are all the animals? (Hiding or indoors.)

WHO'S IN THE BARN?

What you need

Pale buff coloured backing paper, paints, four sets of autumn clothes, guiser's masks (see page 58), root vegetables scooped out to make lanterns (see page 53), ready-made lacy lanterns (see page 55), a green drape, four strong boxes, some straw, large pieces of white drawing paper, felt-tipped pens, scissors, stapler, string, pins, four baskets, a collection of vegetables such as marrows, swedes, parsnips and turnips.

Preparation

Write the sign 'Who's in the barn?' mount it, then staple it onto the display board. Write four more signs 'Marrow', 'Swede', 'Parsnip' and 'Turnip' and mount them each on a piece of folded card.

What to do

Staple the buff coloured sugar paper to the display board. Use corrugated card to make the shape of a barn around the edge of the board. Pin a piece of string across the top of the barn roof and hang up the lacy lanterns. Glue pieces of straw along the bottom of the display.

Place a table in front of the display, and arrange the boxes in a row on the table. Cover the table and boxes with the green drape and pin or tape to the table to secure it. Spread the straw over the table and place the vegetables on the straw. Put an empty basket on top of each box with a vegetable label in front of each one.

Ask four children to lie down on a large sheet of white paper. Draw around their outlines and cut them out. Let the children draw in their facial features, adding string hair. Staple them in a row to the board and add clothes, stapled or pinned into place. Staple a mask onto the top of the head of each body so that it can be lifted up to see whose face is underneath. Put a name label under the mask so that you can easily work out who is beneath it.

Let the children make a flag with their name on it and pin it to their dummy's hand.

Discussion

This display links with the activities 'Punkie lanterns' on page 53, 'Lacy lanterns' on page 55 and 'Guiser's mask' on page 58. Talk about the different vegetables on the display table. Can the children sort them into the correct baskets? Play a guessing game to work out who is hidden behind the masks. What questions do the children need to ask to work out who is hidden?

CHAPTER 8
ASSEMBLIES

This chapter provides ideas for assemblies or group sharing times based upon the theme of 'Autumn'. The aim is to help children to draw upon their past experiences to explore various aspects of thankfulness and includes activities, prayers and songs.

HARVEST TIME

Harvest can be one of the most exciting festivals of the year and is an intrinsic feature of country life in autumn. Encourage the children to understand how fortunate they are to have enough food to eat in order to help them grow and develop in their own special way. They should be aware that people in some countries are not so fortunate and often suffer from malnutrition because there is not enough food for them to eat due to poor harvests and famine.

Introduction

Let the children come into the assembly or sit in a group listening to Vivaldi's *The Four Seasons* 'Autumn' (Concerto No 3). Begin by reading the poem 'Harvest' on page 72 in the Resources section. Encourage the children to think about their favourite food and ask them to make a painting, drawing or model of their favourite food. Collect examples of the chosen foods beforehand.

What to do

Invite the children taking part to stand in a line in front of the group. They could be holding examples of their favourite food to show the other children, or alternatively drawings or models. Encourage the children to describe their favourite food and where it comes from. Explain the importance of varied diet to help them grow properly, pointing out different types of food they could eat. Talk about their good fortune in having so much food to choose from, reminding them that some children have no choice and often feel hungry.

Make some simple biscuits to share at the end of the assembly. Ask one of the children to show the biscuits which they have made to share with the

others in the group. When it is time to share out the biscuits, encourage all the children to say 'thank you' when they receive their biscuit.

Reflection

In silence, ask the children to think about the different people who make food for them. Tell them about the different ways food is provided and prepared for them. Remind them about farmers, factory workers, bakers, shopkeepers, cooks and fishermen, parents and carers who work to bring food to their table on a daily basis. Talk about the harvest of the sea as well as the land and how food has many different sources.

Prayer

Some children may wish to thank God for all the different types of food they have to choose from, that they have enough to eat to enable them to feel satisfied and full and that there is sufficient food to help them grow. They can express thanks for the biscuits they have shared with their friends and thank their parents and carers for providing them with food to eat at meal times.

Song

At the end of the assembly the children could all sing together the song 'Harvest' on page 87 in the Resources section.

SIGHTS OF THE SEASON

In this assembly children are given the opportunity to express their thanks for the beauty of the changing seasons and to become aware of the value of the earth's resources. They will be encouraged to consider how fortunate they are to witness the beautiful colours of autumn and the produce of nature that is in abundance at this time of year. This assembly will work with either a large gathering of children or a small group. It links in well with the activities 'Sense it's autumn' on page 12, 'Shades of autumn' on page 30 and 'Tumbling leaves' on page 33.

Introduction

Begin by making reference to the autumn collection on display and asking the children about their favourite memories of autumn. Describe your own favourite autumn sight to encourage the children to appreciate the beauty of autumn with its changing colours.

Next, read out the poem 'When does autumn begin?' on page 67 in the Resources section, asking the children to take notice of particular aspects of the poem to heighten their awareness of the beauty of the wonderful autumn sights.

What to do

Invite the children to make a collection of objects associated with autumn and display them on a tray or trolley. Ask five children to choose their favourite object from the collection and to think about why they have chosen it. Use the objects to make feely bags by tying each item loosely in an old sock. Stand the children in a line at the front of the group and ask them to hold up the socks for everyone to see. Invite children from the group to come to the front, in turn, to guess what autumn object is hidden in each sock. The children holding objects hidden in the socks can then take them out and hold them up to the rest of the group and say 'This reminds me of autumn because…'. Smaller groups could make an autumn sock each to pass around the circle. Each sock could contain the child's own favourite reminder of autumn which they have collected for themselves.

Reflection

Ask the children to close their eyes and try to imagine what it would be like if they could not see the beautiful collection of autumn objects. Ask them to think about the beautiful shapes and colours of the things on display. As their eyes are closed quietly remind them of the five articles hidden inside the socks. Give the children a few moments silence to contemplate what has been expressed. Encourage them to be aware of how lucky they are to see the beautiful sights of autumn, the changing colours of the season and fruitfulness of nature at this time of year.

Prayer

Some children may like to thank God for the beauty of the autumn season and for the gift of sight to enable them to enjoy what they can see all around them during the colourful months of autumn.

Song

At the end of the activity, the children could all sing together 'Colour me autumn' on page 83 and 'God's wonderful world' on page 86 in the Resources section of this book.

ANIMALS IN AUTUMN

Autumn is an exciting time of the year for children as they sometimes get the chance to glimpse sight of small wild creatures foraging around. The focus of this gathering is to show gratitude for all the creatures that share the earth with us and to hope that they will find an abundance of food from nature's stores to keep them fed throughout the long winter months. Encourage the children to think ahead and prepare special food for the birds so that they will not perish in the cold weather. This assembly ties in well with the activity 'What's in store?' on page 19, 'Fly away' on page 20, 'Hidden seeds' on page 35 and 'Nutty mixtures' on page 38.

Introduction

Begin by explaining about all the things that nature provides for animals to eat during autumn. Talk about the way berries ripen and provide food for birds and other little creatures. Explain that when the bushes and trees are laden with colourful berries, it is a sign that the winter will be harsh. It is nature's way of providing enough food to make sure that the animals survive the long cold months. Explain that although the animals are all different, they still have a special place on God's earth. Tell the story of *The Town Mouse and the Country Mouse* (Traditional) using mice made from the photocopiable sheet on page 91 as props.

What to do

Encourage the children to think of their favourite woodland animal or bird and to practise movement to represent the chosen animal: a mouse could pretend to wipe its whiskers, a robin could shyly hide away underneath its wings. Make simple head masks to make the characters more realistic or, if the group is small, you could dress the children up as woodland animals. If not, choose a few children and ask them to stand at the front with you. In turn, give them the opportunity to explain what animal they are and how they manage to find food and stay warm in autumn.

Reflection

Ask the children to think about ways in which they can help animals and birds to prepare for winter.

Explain that they should strive to care for all the creatures around them, especially those that might be in distress or might be in need of food or warmth. Remind the children to put out food and water for the birds when the weather is very cold. Ask them to leave nature's store cupboard intact by not picking the fruit, nuts and berries so that the animals can find plenty of food for themselves and do not lose their natural hunting instincts.

Prayer

Ask the children to reflect in silence about the true meaning of caring. Ask God to protect the animals from the harsh conditions that arrive with the autumn season, to keep all the animals safe and to provide enough food and warmth so that they will survive the winter months without too much distress. Express thanks for the way we are able to share the earth with the animals and birds, living side by side in harmony.

Song

At the end of the assembly the children could sing the song 'God's wonderful world' on page 86 in the Resources section.

Collective worship in schools

The assemblies outlined here are suitable for use with children in nurseries and playgroups, but would need to be adapted for use with pupils at registered schools. As a result of legislation enacted in 1944, 1988 and 1993, there are now specific points to be observed when developing a programme of Collective Acts of Worship in a school.

Further guidance will be available from your local SACRE – Standing Advisory Council for RE.

POEMS AND ACTION RHYMES

WHO AM I?

I shake the trees.
I blow the smoke.
I empty dustbins
for a joke.

I make the clouds
race in the sky.
I lift your kite
and hold it high.

Who am I?

Celia Warren

WHEN DOES AUTUMN BEGIN?

How do we know when autumn's here?
Here are the signs that autumn's near:

Sleepy birds will fly away
And not return 'til warmer days

Leaves will change from green to red
And start to fall around your head

Conkers grow on horse chestnut trees
A cold wind blows around your knees

Animals are safe and sound
In burrows hidden underground

Woolly hats and scarves appear
Bonfire night is drawing near

The clearest sign that summer's lost
Is autumn's first white, crunchy frost

Autumn starts with many things
Robins, fireworks, harvest hymns

How do we know when autumn's near?
All these things says that autumn's here!

Kirsty Bilton

PHOTOCOPIABLE RESOURCES

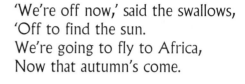

FLYING AWAY

'We're off now,' said the swallows,
'Off to find the sun.
We're going to fly to Africa,
Now that autumn's come.

We're sorry to be going,
But we have to leave you here.
Watch out for us returning
To these parts again next year.'

(Can you pretend that your hands are
birds flying?)

Susan Eames

SQUIRREL STORE

(A counting rhyme)

1 nut, 2 nuts,
3 nuts, 4.
Squirrels go gathering
a winter store.

5 nuts, 6 nuts,
7 nuts, 8.
Leaves are falling
so they mustn't be late.

9 nuts, 10 nuts,
here comes the snow.
A scurry and a skip
and away they go!

Tony Mitton

ONE LITTLE HEDGEHOG

One little hedgehog
Hiding in the leaves,
Snuffle snuffle, sniff sniff,
Tickle, wriggle, sneeze.

Actions

This is a simple counting rhyme. Increase the
number of hedgehogs as you wish. Children have
to hold up the correct number of fingers. The
children sneeze after they say the word 'sneeze',
between each verse.)

Coral Rumble

AUTUMN CARPET

Leaves are falling
In the street,
To make a carpet
For our feet.
One leaf,
Two leaves,
Three leaves,
Four!
Wind blows stronger –
HUNDREDS more!
Crisp and crunchy
Shades of brown,
An autumn carpet
Cloaks the town!

Trevor Harvey

PHOTOCOPIABLE RESOURCES

HERE ARE THE TREES

Here are the trees
so leafy and tall.

(Stand with arms up as branches, hands and fingers extended.)

Look at the leaves
as they shrivel and fall.

(Curl up hands, then use them to show leaves falling down towards ground.)

Listen and hear
what a whispery sound...

(Place hand to ear to suggest listening. Some children can make whispery noises too.)

they make as they flutter
and float to the ground.

(Bring leaf-hands right down to rest on floor for brief pause.)

Here are the branches,
so naked and plain,

(Stand and extend arms again, this time with fists closed and arms slightly drawn in.)

waiting for Spring
when the leaves grow again.

(Open hands to show fingers stretching out. Push arms out a little to emphasize gesture.)

Tony Mitton

SYCAMORE SEED

Sycamore, sycamore,
Summer has gone.
Leave your tree
and fly for a home!

Sycamore, sycamore,
nights draw in.
Slip from the branch
and spread your wing!

Sycamore, sycamore,
spin to land,
writing your name
on the Autumn wind.

Judith Nicholls

DANDELION WHISPERS

Dandelion seeds
Float like
Fairy dust,
Whispering white,
Tickling the air.

Coral Rumble

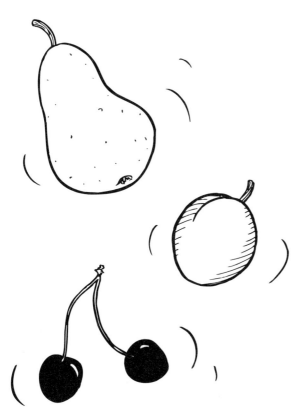

THE FRUIT RHYME

Apple, cherry,
pear and plum,
ripe and juicy,
here they come.

Fill your basket
cram your bowl.
Watch them tumble,
see them roll.

Autumn fruits
are plump and sweet.
Come and try them.
Pick and eat.

Tony Mitton

I'M A LITTLE CONKER!

I'm a little conker,
Shiny, brown,
And I've just come
Tumbling down!
Here I lie
Upon the ground
Bursting, waiting
To be found!

Sue Cowling

AUTUMN BONFIRE

Crackle, sputter, mutter, hiss,
Golden sparks flash out and fly.
Red hot cheeks from glowing branches.
Flames alight in stinging eyes.
Smell the woodsmoke, listen to this
Crackle, sputter, mutter, hiss.

Penny Kent

HARVEST

Gather the fish
From out of the seas.
Pick the fruit
From off the trees.

Cut down the corn
To make our bread.
Milk the cows
In the cattle shed.

Make the butter
And the cheese.
Bottle the jam
And freeze the peas.

Dig potatoes
Carrots and more,
Put the onions
Into store.

Share the Harvest
Give thanks together
For harvest saved
And Autumn weather.

Brenda Williams

APPLE BOBBING

Water in the barrel
Water up my nose
Water on my hair
Water on my clothes

Apples in the water
Bobbing underneath
Apples in the barrel
But not between my teeth!

Brenda Williams

PHOTOCOPIABLE RESOURCES

LANTERNS

Now's the time
    for paper lanterns
      hanging
        in the air
gently swaying,
    lightly playing,
      glowing
        everywhere:

Delicate
    and brightly coloured,
      bobbing
        in the breeze
like a lot
    of magic flowers...
      Come and look
        at these!

See them bring
    their vivid colours
      to the darkened
        trees,
orange, pink
    and primrose yellow.
      Let me hold one –
        please!

Jean Kenward

NEW TASTE FESTIVAL

Rice is sown,
Rice has grown,
Now it's harvest –
Time has flown!

Stay up late,
Celebrate,
See how hard work
Fills your plate!

Sue Cowling

STORIES

MRS RABBIT'S AUTUMN PIE

Mrs Rabbit popped her head out of her back door and sniffed. Twitch, twitch, twitch went her nose and whiskers.

There was a cold mist hanging over the bracken, and spiders' webs hung like little necklaces strung with beads of dew. The air was quite nippy.

'Swallows will be flying off today,' she said to herself, looking up at the rows of chattering birds sitting on the telegraph wires. 'It's time for Autumn Pie!'

'Yeah! Autumn Pie!' shrieked her three kittens, Nob, Bob and Lopears. They had scrambled out of bed when they heard their mother about. Autumn Pie was their very favourite treat.

'First, I need you to help me plant my bulbs,' said Mrs Rabbit.

'Oww!' cried the kittens. This was not what they wanted at all.

'No bulbs, no pie!' said their mother.

The rabbits all planted bulbs. Dig, dig, dig. Daffodils, crocuses, tulips and snowdrops. In the garden, round the house and in the window boxes. Mrs Rabbit wanted their home to look very pretty in the Spring when all the bulbs would flower.

'There now,' said Mrs Rabbit. 'That should do it.'

'Autumn Pie!' shrieked the children.

'Now we have to clear the leaves,' she said.

'Oww!' cried the kittens. This was not what they wanted, either.

'No leaves, no pie!' said her mother.

The rabbits took their brooms made of twigs and swept away the leaves round the house. Sweep, sweep, sweep. Soon they had a great pile of leaves pushed tidily between the big trees behind the house.

'There now,' said Mrs Rabbit. 'That should do it.'

'Autumn Pie!' shrieked the children.

'Now we have to fetch some wood,' she said.

'Oww!' cried the kittens. They didn't want to fetch wood.

'No wood, no pie!' said their mother.

In amongst the trees went the rabbits, picking up fallen twigs and tying them into bundles ready for carrying. Huff, puff, puff. They stacked the wood next to the stove, ready for making a fire.

'There now,' said Mrs Rabbit. 'That should do it.'

'Autumn Pie!' shrieked the children.

'We'll have to pick the fruit,' she said.

'Oww!' cried the kittens. It sounded like more hard work.

'No fruit, no pie,' said their mother.

Off to the orchard they went. Nob filled the basket with windfalls. Munch, munch, munch. Then they went among the soft-fruit canes. Bob filled his basket with raspberries and blackberries. Munch, munch, munch. Finally, Mrs Rabbit took them behind the kitchen garden. Lopears filled her basket with peaches and apricots from the fruit trees growing along the wall. Munch, munch, munch.

'There now,' said Mrs Rabbit. 'That should do it.'

'Mmm, mmm, mmm!' mumbled her children. Their mouths were full of fruit and they were covered in stains.

'We'll have to make the pastry now!' she said.

'Oww!' grumbled the kittens. More work!

'No pastry, no pie,' said their mother.

Into the bowl went flour, butter, sugar and milk. Nob, Bob and Lopears took turns to rub them all together and roll out the pastry on the kitchen table. They filled the pie tin with all the chopped up fruit they had gathered and plenty of sugar. Carefully they put the crust on top.

'There now,' said Mrs Rabbit. 'That should do it.'

'Autumn Pie!' said her children.

'Not quite,' said their mother. 'Now we have to bake it.'

'Oww!' said the kittens. How much longer did they have to wait?

'No baking, no pie,' said their mother.

The sun dropped low in the sky. It grew dark early now. Mrs Rabbit took one last look in the oven.

Yes, the pie was ready. The kitchen was filled with delicious smells.

She put on her oven gloves, took out the precious pie and stood it on a mat on the table. The crust was a wonderful golden colour.

'Time for Autumn Pie!' she called. But there was no reply.

Nob, Bob and Lopears had worked so hard, and had eaten so much fruit, that they were all fast asleep.

Mrs Rabbit smiled. 'Well, I think I'll just have a piece myself.'

She cut a piece of pie, poured cream over the top, and sat in her favourite armchair by the fire to eat it. She thought about all the good work they had done that day: the bulbs were planted, the leaves were swept and the wood was gathered.

Her Autumn Pie tasted particularly good that year.

Jackie Andrews

FALLING LEAVES

One misty Autumn morning, Mr Fox went to open the door to the earth and found it blocked with leaves. After much pushing and shoving, the door swung open.

'Just look at all this mess!' grumbled Mr Fox, his bushy tail waving crossly. 'It'll take me ages to sweep all these up.'

Young Tom Fox followed his dad into the misty sunshine. All round the hill where they lived, the ground was covered with red, brown, orange and yellow leaves. 'Oh, wow!' he said, tossing them into the air with his paws. 'Where have these all come from?'

'They've fallen off the trees,' Mr Fox told him.

Tom looked up and saw that the branches of the trees around them were all bare, apart from a few leaves here and there still hanging on.

'Why have they fallen? And why aren't they green any more?'

'Many trees sort of go to sleep in the winter,' explained Mr Fox. 'The sap inside their trunks stops flowing upwards, and this makes the leaves change colour and die. Then in Spring, when the sap rises again, new green leaves appear.'

His eyes wide with wonder, Tom stared up at the trees then down at the carpet of leaves on the floor. He touched them with his nose.

'Aren't they beautiful!' he said, and he pounced on a particularly large, yellow chestnut leaf.

'Huh!' snorted Mr Fox as he raked the leaves away from their door. 'They might look nice, but they make a lot of work! Mrs Fox won't want all these cluttering up the path.'

Suddenly, another leaf fluttered just above Tom's head. He swatted it with his paws, trying to catch it, but the wind blew it away again. Tom chased the leaf down the hillside until it finally landed on the ground. He caught the leaf in his mouth and rolled over and over, pretending to fight it.

Then Tom saw other leaves falling from the trees in the wood and he chased after them, this way and that, not noticing how far into the wood they were taking him. The leaves swirled and twirled through the air, tumbling to the ground before he could grab them.

Then an oak leaf fluttered just in front of his nose.

'Got you!' Tom snapped it with his sharp little teeth, barking with excitement. But the sound was strange. Muffled. Quiet.

Holding the leaf down with his paw, Tom turned around. To his dismay, the mist had filled the spaces between the trees and his home was nowhere in sight. The fallen leaves

covered the ground so completely, they hid the path.

'Dad?' he called, his voice trembly. There was no answering call. Tom ran this way and that way, trying to find the way home. But he just got more and more lost. Tired, cold and frightened, he curled up between some tree roots, his nose tucked under his bushy tail.

The wind rustled the tree's branches and a colourful shower of leaves fluttered down. They fell gently over Tom, covering him like a blanket and keeping him warm.

Tom fell asleep.

And that's how Mr Fox found him.

'Tom!' he cried. 'I've been looking for you everywhere!'

'I was chasing the leaves and I got lost,' Tom explained, as he shook himself free of his leafy nest. 'But look, the leaves kept me warm.'

Mr Fox grinned. 'Well, I'm very glad they did. But you must promise not to wander so far from home on your own again. Mrs Fox was very worried, you know. Come on, let's go get some dinner. It smells like her best roast chicken and potatoes.'

'Yum!' said Tom, running ahead. Chasing leaves made a young fox cub *very* hungry!

Karen King

PHOTOCOPIABLE RESOURCES

JAKE'S TREE

A huge oak tree grew in the field behind Jake's house.

On summer days Jake and his mum sometimes had a picnic underneath it. Jake liked the cool shade the tree made. He liked the way the wind whispered in the leaves. But most of all he liked the low-hanging branches. There was nothing he wanted more than to swing from them. But even when he stood on tiptoe and stretched up really hard, he just couldn't reach.

'Will I ever be big enough?' Jake asked his mum.

'Of course you will,' she laughed. 'Maybe next year. This old tree's been growing for hundreds of years. You'll have to be patient.'

When autumn came, it was too cold for picnics, but Jake and his mum still went for walks in the field. The leaves on the oak tree gradually turned orange, yellow and brown before falling to the ground. Jake liked to scrunch through them in his boots.

One afternoon, as he kicked through the leaves under the tree, Jake noticed something else on the ground. They looked like small brown nuts in little cups.

'What are these?' he asked Mum, holding one out.

'They're acorns,' said Mum. 'They are the seeds from the oak tree. There's a tree inside each one of them.'

Jake stared at the small acorn, and then up at the huge tree towering over them. It didn't seem possible. 'How does it fit inside?' he asked.

Jake's mum laughed. 'Remember those sunflower seeds you planted last spring? They were small seeds that grew into tall plants when you put them in the garden. Well acorns are just like that. They will lie in the ground all winter, and in spring they will start to grow into new oak trees.'

PHOTOCOPIABLE RESOURCES

Jake looked at the ground around them. He saw a small bare patch of earth. Taking a twig, he worked at the soil until it was soft and crumbly, then he pushed his acorn into the hole and covered it over with soil and leaves, patting it down carefully.

'There!' he said. 'I've planted one. Will it take long to grow?'

'I'm afraid so,' said his mum. 'You'll have to be patient.'

Jake was patient. He waited for weeks, but nothing happened. The days got colder, and as winter came Jake stopped going to the tree. He forgot all about the acorn.

In the spring, Jake noticed the new green leaves appearing on the trees and shrubs in their garden. In the field, the oak tree, too, had a greenish look to it. Jake asked his mum if he had grown tall enough to reach the lower branches.

'Let's go and see,' she said.

They went over the stile and across the grassy meadow. As Jake ran over to the tree, he could see clearly the new leaves unfolding from every twig. He reached the lowest branch and stretched up on tiptoe, with his arms above his head. He was still just too short, but perhaps...

Jake jumped as high as he could and managed to grasp the branch. He swung to and fro until his arms ached and he had to drop down to the ground again.

As he landed he spotted a shoot poking up through a bare patch of soil. It had a couple of pale new leaves at the top. Jake suddenly remembered his acorn. It *had* grown after all!

'Mum! Look!' he cried.

He knelt down and looked at the tiny oak. How would it ever grow as tall as the big tree? Then he thought of himself last summer, trying to reach the branches.

'You'll have to be patient,' he told the little shoot, 'and maybe by next year you'll be as big as me.'

Jillian Harker

SONGS

MISTER AUTUMN

Clive Barnwell

SIGNS OF AUTUMN

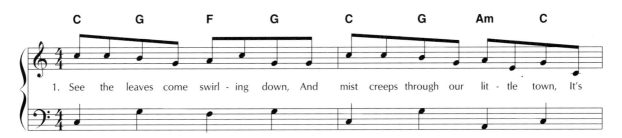

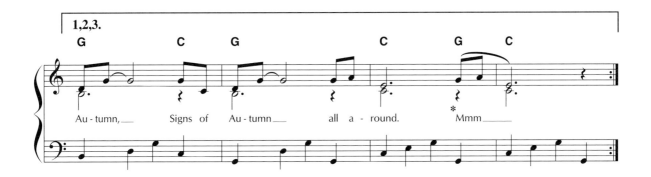

*These 'echo' phrases could be played on any tuned instrument,
chime bars, glockenspiel, xylophone etc.

2. Frosty days are here again
There's steam upon the window pane,
It's Autumn,
Signs of Autumn – down the lane (mmm).

3. Bonfires tinge the evening air
And fireworks bang and children stare,
It's Autumn,
Signs of Autumn – everywhere (mmm).

4. Birds migrating every day
And dormice want to hide away,
It's Autumn,
Yes it's Autumn – come and play! (mmm)

Verses 1, 2, 3 – notes G A E

Verse 4 – notes G E C

Jean Gilbert

PHOTOCOPIABLE RESOURCES

PICK! PLUCK! PULL!

Down in the or-chard there's work to be done, And if we all go___ we'll have some fun. There's lots of *ap-ples hang-ing on the tree, The bran-ches are as hea-vy as___ can be.

Chorus

Pick! Pluck! Pull! all the *ap-ples off the tree. Lots for you and___ lots for me! Pick! Pluck! Pull! 'til the bas-ket's full.

1,2,3,4. Shall we eat some for our tea? Mmm. **5.** tea? Mmm. Yum! Yum!

Actions:

Mime a tree with arms. Lower arms to show heavy branches, laden with lots of fruit.

Mime picking the fruit, 'Pick, pluck, pull!' bits, and mime a tree with your arms again. Point for 'you' and 'me'.

Mime the outline of a loaded basket.

And finally pretend to bite into the fruit.

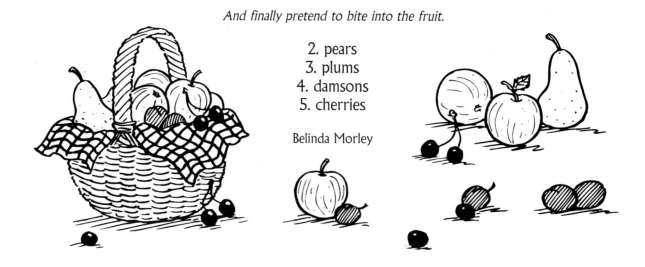

2. pears
3. plums
4. damsons
5. cherries

Belinda Morley

COLOUR ME AUTUMN

| D | | | G | Em | | F♯m | | Bm |
Red and yel - low, or - ange brown and gold, Now it's get - ting cold

| Em | A | D | G | Em |
col - our me Au - tumn. Red and yel - low or - ange gold and brown,

| F♯m | Bm | Em | A | D |
When the leaves fall down, co - lour me Au - tumn do.

Clive Barnwell

TIME TO SAY GOODBYE

1. The mar-tins a-bove are whisp'-ring, "It's au-tumn so we must fly," The barn owl wise-ly nods his head, "It's time to say good-bye."

2. The swallows above...
3. The cuckoos above...

Ann Bryant

ONE LITTLE ACORN

1. One day in Au - tumn, I found, One lit - tle a - corn ly - ing on the ground.

Optional ostinato

2. One day in autumn, I found
One little acorn,
Two little beech nuts,
Lying on the ground.

3. One day in autumn, I found,
One little acorn,
Two little beech nuts,
Three little conkers
Lying on the ground.

Susan Eames

PHOTOCOPIABLE RESOURCES

GOD'S WONDERFUL WORLD

What can I see when I close my eyes? God's won-der-ful world.

What can I see when I close my eyes? God's won-der-ful world.

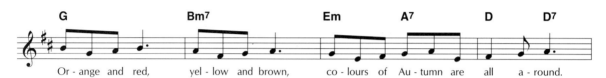

Or-ange and red, yel-low and brown, co-lours of Au-tumn are all a-round.

Trees look so sad when they lose their leaves, But God will make sure there are more next year.

Peter Morrell

THEMES
for early years

HARVEST

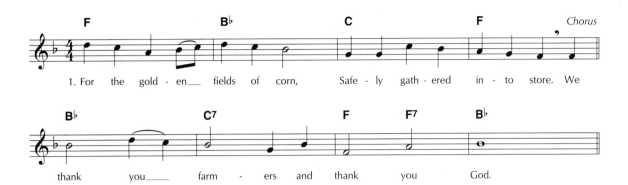

1. For the gold - en— fields of corn, Safe - ly gath - ered in - to store. We

thank you— farm - ers and thank you God.

2. For the orchards full of fruit
Grown with care for us to eat
Chorus

3. For the hedgerow's fruit and nuts
Shared by birds and beasts and us
Chorus

4. For the oceans full of fish
Caught and brought ashore for us
Chorus

5. For the food we find in stores
Harvested around the world
Chorus

6. For the harvest gathered in
That the whole world may be fed
Chorus

7. For our world that we may all
Take good care of nature's gifts
Chorus

Carole Henderson-Begg

THEMES
for early years

Name _____

Light up the sky

Draw a line to match each firework to its cloudburst.
Colour the fireworks in bright colours.

THEMES
for early years

Food for squirrel

Cut out the pictures and put them in the correct order. Match the acorns to the correct sized tree.

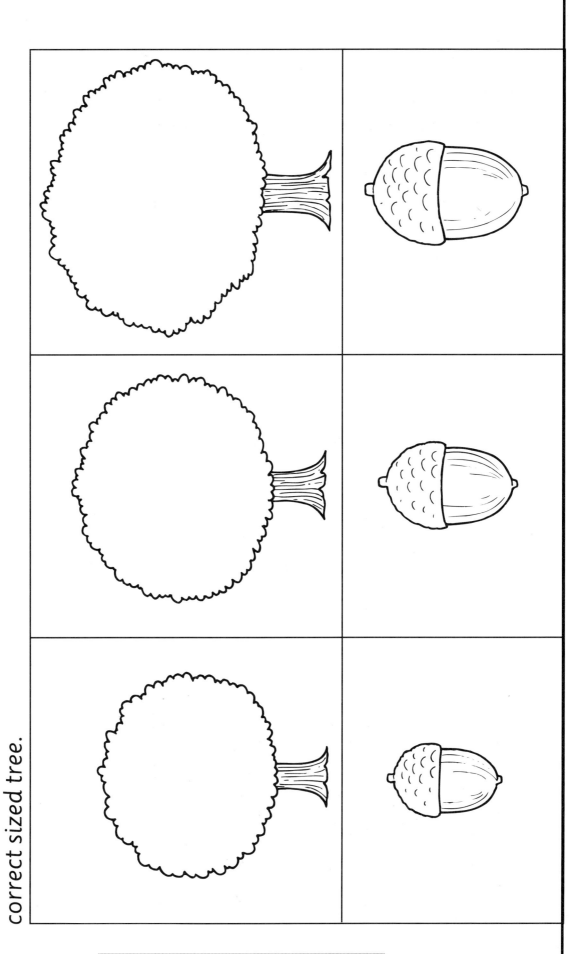

Make a bird kite

Decorate your bird with feathers. Cut around the outline and fold along the dotted lines. Tie some thread through the hole to make a flying bird 'kite'.

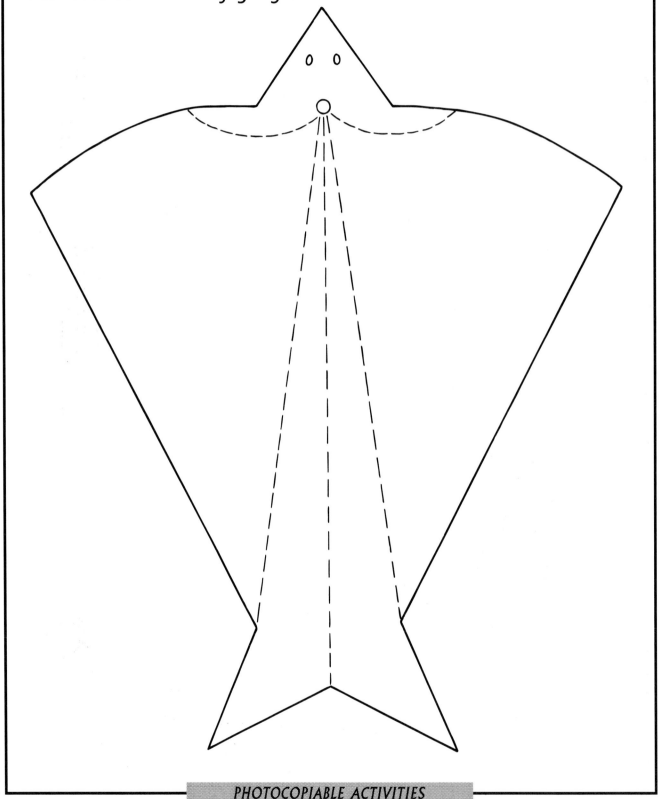

THEMES
for early years

Finger mouse puppet

Decorate the mouse puppet then cut along the lines. Fold along the dotted lines and tape the two long sides together. Add whiskers to your mouse's nose.

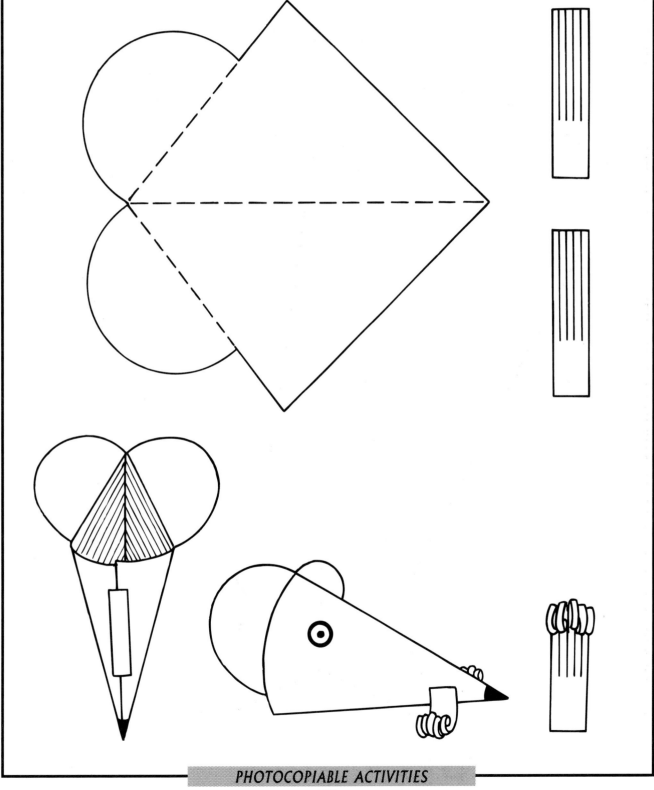

THEMES
for early years

Autumn animals

Name _____

THEMES
for early years

Name _____

Colourful leaves

Use the colour code to colour in the leaves. Throw a dice and move your counter to the correct colour.

Colour code
1   Yellow
2   Brown
3   Red
4   Green

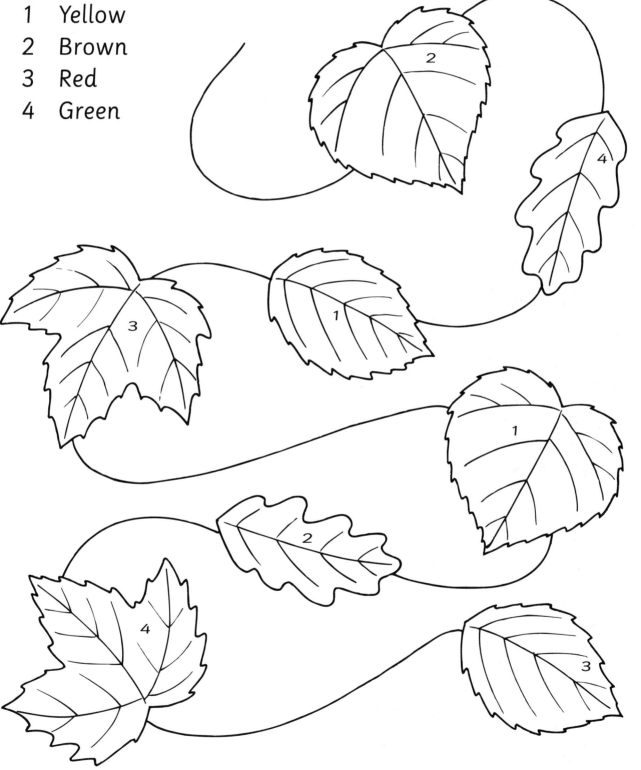

THEMES
for early years

Name _____

Rangoli patterns

Stick autumn seeds on the shapes to make a Rangoli pattern.

THEMES
for early years

Paper lantern

Decorate the lantern with autumn colours.
Cut along the dotted lines. Fold the shaded
ends in and glue together. Add a handle made
from string then hang up your lantern.

fold along here

THEMES
for early years

RECOMMENDED MATERIALS

SONG BOOKS
Apusskidu – Songs for children (A & C Black)
Game-songs With Prof Dogg's Troupe Harriet Powell (A & C Black)
Okki-tokki-unga (A & C Black)
Harlequin: 44 Songs For Round the Year (A & C Black)

POEMS, RHYMES AND PRAYERS
Book of Prayers David Palmer (Ladybird)
A Year Full of Stories 366 Stories and Poems Georgia Adams and Selina Young (Orion)
The Oxford Dictionary of Nursery Rhymes Iona and Peter Opie (OUP)
The Young Puffin Book of Verse compiled by Barbara Ireson (Puffin) (Out of print)
This Little Puffin compiled by Elizabeth Matterson (Puffin)

PICTURE AND STORY BOOKS
A Year Full of Stories 366 Stories and Poems Georgia Adams and Selina Young (Orion)
Festivals Together: 'The Boggart' Fitzjohn, Weston and Large (Hawthorne Press)
Hansel and Gretel Traditional (Ladybird)
Postman Pat's Foggy Day John Cunliffe (Hippo Books)
The Owl's Lesson Nick Butterworth (Harper Collins)
The Town Mouse and The Country Mouse Traditional (Ladybird)
The Very Hungry Caterpillar Eric Carle (Hamish Hamilton)
What Will the Weather be Like Today? Paul Kazuko Roger (Orchard Books)
Out and About Shirley Hughes (Walker Books)

INFORMATION BOOKS
Animal Homes Gillian Dorfman (Ladybird books)
Autumn Story Jill Barklem (Harper Collins)
'The Seasons' Topic Box series Clare Llewellyn (Wayland)
'Autumn' Seasons Around You series Saviour Pirotta (Wayland)
Autumn on the farm Jillian Powell (Wayland)

'Autumn' *Seasonal Crafts* series Gillian Chapman (Wayland)
My First Green Book Angela Wilkes (Dorling Kindersley)

TEACHERS' BOOK
'Autumn & Winter Festivals' *Themes for Early Years* series Carole Court (Scholastic)

MUSIC
'Troyte' from *Enigma Variations* by Elgar
'Sparks' from *Tommy* by The Who
'Ce qu'a vu le vent d'Ouest' by Debussey
'Mars' from *The Planets* by Holst

OTHER RESOURCES
'Bread', filmstrip by Philip Green Educational Ltd, 112a Alcester Road, Studley, Warwickshire B80 7NR
Pictorial Charts Educational Trust, 27 Kirchen Road, London W13 0UD
Religion in Evidence, TTS Ltd, Unit 7, Monk Road, Alfreton, Derbyshire, DE55 7RL – information on Muslim beliefs and festivals
Royal Society for the Protection of Birds, The Lodge, Sandy, Bedfordshire SG19 2DL
Royal Society for the Prevention of Cruelty to Animals, Manor House, Causeway, Horsham, West Sussex RH12 1HG

PHOTOCOPIABLE RESOURCES